God and Evil

God and Evil

An Introduction to the Issues

Michael L. Peterson
ASBURY COLLEGE

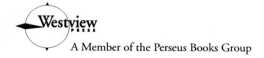

A Member of the Perseus Books Group

Copyright © 1998 by Westview Press, A Member of Perseus Books Group

Published in 1998 in the United States of America by Westview Press, 5500 Central Avenue, Boulder, Colorado 80301-2877, and in the United Kingdom by Westview Press, 12 Hid's Copse Road, Cumnor Hill, Oxford OX2 9JJ

Library of Congress Cataloging-in-Publication Data
Peterson, Michael L. 1950–
  God and evil : an introduction to the issues / by Michael L.
Peterson.
      p. cm.
  Includes bibliographical references and index.
  ISBN 0-8133-2848-9 (hc). — ISBN 0-8133-2849-7 (pb)
  1. Good and evil.   2. Religion—Philosophy.   I. Title.
BJ1401.P47   1998
214—dc21   98-18429
                                                                              CIP

The paper used in this publication meets the requirements of the American National Standard for Permanence of Paper for Printed Library Materials Z39.48-1984.

10   9   8   7   6   5   4

For my sons,
Aaron and Adam

Contents

Preface

This volume is an introduction to the problem of evil as it is currently discussed in professional philosophy. I have designed the book for use in an academic setting, with hopes that both student and scholar may find many points interesting and provocative. I also trust that the serious and thoughtful person outside academia may benefit from my treatment of this perennially important subject.

No project of this sort is a purely private undertaking. Over the years, I have benefited from helpful discussions on the problem of evil with Alvin Plantinga, Edward Madden, Peter Hare, William Hasker, David Basinger, Bruce Reichenbach, and Jerry Walls. I have appreciated the encouragement of the Asbury College administration during my writing. I am also thankful to Pew Charitable Trusts for funding my research during the 1992–1993 academic year.

I am not completely sure why I continue to be fascinated by the problem of evil in all of its permutations. In part, I am astonished by the great profusion of suffering and evil around us and am driven to ponder it on behalf of those who ask, "Why?" And, in part, I am staggered at the capacity for evil within us and am thereby drawn to the issues concerning God and evil. Although I am conscious of the strange mixture of good and evil in our world, I am more mindful of how important it is to orient oneself properly toward these realities.

I dedicate this book to my sons, Aaron and Adam, in whom I take great pleasure and delight. They are certainly two immeasurable goods in my life that show me just how much value there is in a world that contains evil. Their goodness even makes me a better person. My fatherly hope for them is that they will resist evil in all its forms and that they will love and seek the good in all things.

Michael L. Peterson

1

The Problem of Evil and
Its Place in Philosophy of Religion

Something is dreadfully wrong with our world. An earthquake kills hundreds in Peru. A pancreatic cancer patient suffers prolonged, excruciating pain and dies. A pit bull attacks a two-year-old child, angrily ripping his flesh and killing him. Countless multitudes suffer the ravages of war in Somalia. A crazed cult leader pushes eighty-five people to their deaths in Waco, Texas. Millions starve and die in North Korea as famine ravages the land. Horrible things of all kinds happen in our world—and that has been the story since the dawn of civilization. Today's news media thrive on things that are wrong in the world, on bad things that happen to people every day. Television parades vivid images of war, murder, devastation, and suffering before our eyes. Newspapers report rape, abuse, mayhem, and disaster.

Evil in Human Existence

In June 1991, *Time* magazine asked the question, "Why?"—"Why does evil happen?"[1] In the cover essay, journalist Lance Morrow reviews the multitude of evils that haunt our consciousness—from Hitler's Auschwitz to Saddam Hussein's invasion of Kuwait, from KKK hangings of black men in pre–civil rights Mississippi to the AIDS epidemic. Right there in a popular magazine, Morrow raises age-old questions in an article starkly titled "Evil." Is evil an entity? Or is evil the immoral and inhumane actions of persons? What about bad and hurtful things that are out of our control, such as disease, floods, and mental illness? Is nature responsible? Why does evil seem so fascinating and alluring to the human mind while good seems so uninteresting and boring? Does evil serve some purpose, or does it just happen? Why has the human race not seemed able to understand evil, to conquer it, to shut it out?

Thoughtful people raise penetrating questions about evil and seek to understand what it reveals about the human condition. In a feature article in the *New York Times Magazine,* Ron Rosenbaum seeks to probe the meaning of evil. The cover of the magazine reads "Evil's Back," and Rosenbaum's article inside carries the title "Staring into the Heart of the Heart of Darkness." Rosenbaum's piece sets the stage by recounting how Susan Smith of Buffalo, South Carolina, murdered her two young sons. He rehearses the facts that a whole nation now knows all too well: Susan Smith drowned her two little boys by strapping them into the child safety seats in her Mazda and sending the car rolling down an embankment into John D. Long Lake. She then manufactured an "ordeal" to deflect attention from her crime. Playing on racial prejudice, she claimed that an African American car jacker had kidnapped her two children, and she pled desperately on television for a search for the car jacker and the children. Yet, within nine days, she confessed to killing three-year-old Michael and fourteen-month-old Alex.

Rosenbaum observes that one local tabloid called Smith's action an "evil deed." What is impressive about this pronouncement is that the secular news media would make it. In a day when electronic and printed media typically prefer to assume a "relativity of values"— avoiding difficult issues about morality, theology, the meaning of life, and our place in the cosmos—it was blurted out. There it was. Something was actually declared "evil"—pure, unadulterated, unmistakable evil—by the press. Now all the hard questions are laid on the table and have to be faced: What is evil? Why do humans have the seemingly vast capacity to harm others? If there is a good God, why does he permit innocent people to suffer?[2]

There is something about the Susan Smith case that evokes our harshest moral judgments and gets us asking all of those hard questions. Rosenbaum cannily observes that "the great tabloid stories are the ones that raise theological questions." Yet he quickly acknowledges that we cannot talk about evil—or about good, for that matter—without some definitions. Those definitions lead us to larger theories about the origin and existence of evil in our midst, and those theories lead us to even larger conceptions of the meaning of life and the nature of whatever Supreme Being might exist.[3]

Although our age is acutely conscious of the widespread existence of evil in human life, past ages have certainly been aware of its profound significance. Almost no other theme recurs in great literature more often than that of humanity's capability for evil. In ancient Greek tragedy, for example, the tragic hero is a person of noble status and lofty aspirations who is eventually undone because of a profound character flaw, known as *hubris* (pride). All of the tragic hero's other virtues become disjointed as his flaw subtly ruins his life. Russian author Fyodor Dostoevsky treats scornfully the comforting notion that humans are always rational and good. In a famous passage from *The Brothers Karamazov*, Dostoevsky protests such wild optimism about humankind: "I can't endure that a man of lofty mind and heart begins with the ideal of the Madonna and ends with the ideal of Sodom. What's still more awful is that a man with the ideal of Sodom in his soul does not renounce the ideal of the Madonna, and his heart may be on fire with that ideal, genuinely on fire, just as in the days of youth and innocence."[4] Our human inability to live up to our own high ideals is a perpetual puzzlement.

The paradoxical depravity and perversity of humanity are treated quite poignantly in *Dr. Jekyll and Mr. Hyde*. Robert Louis Stevenson's frightening fable records how the decent Dr. Jekyll came under the power of a transforming drug: "It severed in me those provinces of good and ill which divide and compound man's dual nature. I was in no sense a hypocrite; both sides of me were in dead earnest; I was no more myself when I laid aside restraint and plunged in shame, than when I labored, in the eye of day, at the furtherance of knowledge or the relief of sorrow and suffering."[5]

As time went on, the thought of evil represented in the person of Mr. Hyde no longer filled Jekyll with terror: "I sat in the sun on a bench; the animal within me licking the chops of memory; the spiritual side a little drowsed, promising subsequent penitence, but not yet moved to begin. I began to be aware of the temper of my thoughts, a greater boldness, a contempt of danger, a solution of the bonds of obligation."[6]

The apelike creature had diabolically gained control of Jekyll:

This was the shocking thing; that the slime of the pit seemed to utter cries and voices; that the amorphous dust gesticulated and sinned; that what was dead, and had no shape, should usurp the offices of life. And this again, that the insurgent horror was knit to him closer than a wife, closer than an eye; lay caged in his flesh, where he heard it mutter and felt it struggle to be born; and at every hour of weakness, and in the confidence of slumber prevailed against him, and deposed him out of life.[7]

Dr. Jekyll confesses the terrible truth that he is radically both natures: "It was the curse of mankind that . . . in the agonized womb of consciousness these polar twins should be continuously struggling."[8]

Paul, the early Christian evangelist, recognizes the war within himself: "I do not understand my own actions. For I do not do what I want, but I do the very thing I hate. . . . I can will what is right, but I cannot do it. For I do not do the good I want, but the evil I do not want is what I do."[9] In a similar vein, St. Augustine recounts his unhappy predicament in his *Confessions*: "I was bound, not with another's irons, but by my own iron will. My will the enemy held, and thence had made a chain for me, and bound me."[10] This personal aspect of evil most closely coincides with what the Judeo-Christian Scriptures describe as "sin."

Once we recognize the existence of something that can reasonably be called personal evil, we must then also recognize that it has collective as well as individual dimensions. Organized crime syndicates, militant emerging nations, oppressive social structures, and profit-crazed multinational corporations are, in a real sense, the social extensions of personal evil. On both individual and corporate levels, one of the saddest features of human evil is its strange admixture with good or apparent good. Marriages are wrecked for lack of mutual understanding, educational communities are undermined by disagreement about how to pursue common ideals, political parties are thrown into disarray by excessive ambition, and nations are ripped apart by struggles for power.

Although we are perplexed by humanity's capacity for evil, even the best of us are sometimes hurt and even crushed by the impersonal forces of the universe. These forces know nothing of human agendas or purposes and tend to thwart all that we hold dear. Herman Melville deals with this theme in *Moby Dick*. Captain Ahab of the *Pequod,* forty years a whaler in the first half of the last century, sets out from Nantucket on what appears to be a long whaling cruise. Little does anyone know that Ahab's journey is not seaman's business but a quest for the meaning of life. Ahab had lost a leg in an earlier encounter with Moby Dick, a great white whale, then the terror of the seas, and is now bent on destroying it. The captain is obsessed with the meaning of human existence in the face of overwhelming natural forces. Ironically, the whale is white, a color often taken to symbolize what is sacred and holy; but the whale is fearsome and hostile to human values and, in the end, triumphant. Ishmael, the ship's only survivor, claims that in losing his life Ahab discovered its meaning.[11] The modern world knows all too well that this disturbing picture of life—life being ruined and finally snuffed out by forces beyond its control—is a realistic one.

There is no denying that persons often fall victim to psychological and physical forces beyond their control. But quite apart from how these forces affect human interests, they certainly cause much pain and death within nature itself. As Alfred Lord Tennyson reminds us, nature is "red in tooth and claw." Survival of the fittest is built into the mechanism of animate nature. Few animals are free from attack by stronger animals or from suffering and death due to shifts in their environment. Although animals do not possess the higher self-consciousness of humans, they still obviously feel pain and endure suffering. Thoughtful people find it very puzzling that the world should work in such a way as to maim, torture, and destroy large proportions of these subhuman creatures.

At the end of any catalog of ills that plague the world comes death. All things eventually die. But death is a particularly acute problem for the human species because we humans sense that our existence has value and worth, that our agendas have merit, that we deserve to go on living and building our lives. And yet death stands as the final enemy, the last evil we must face; it puts an end not only to our doing and undergoing further evils but also to our pursuing our most cherished dreams. Thus, death is radically foreign to all that is within us. Ludwig Wittgenstein observes: "Death is not an event in life: we do not live to experience death."[12] Death is the end of life. H. F. Lovell Cocks writes that the termination of one's own personal existence is the "great human repression, the universal 'complex.' Dying is the reality that [persons] dare not face, and to escape which [they] summon all [their] resources."[13] Those who have thought long and hard about the human condition know that death is arguably the most fearsome of all evils.

After pondering evil in the world, we may be tempted to echo the sentiment in the chorus of T. S. Eliot's *Murder in the Cathedral*:

> *Here is no continuing city, here*
> *is no abiding stay.*
> *Ill the wind, ill the time, uncertain*
> *the profit, certain the danger.*

> *O late late late, late is the time,*
> *too late, and rotten the year;*
> *Evil the wind, and bitter the sea, and*
> *grey the sky, grey grey grey.*[14]

Unfortunately, this profound and inconsolable pessimism appears to be natural and warranted when the troubles of humanity are taken seriously.

All of the bad things that happen—horrors that we human beings commit toward one another, awful events that occur in nature, and terrifying ways in which nature threatens human interests—fall under the rubric of evil. Simply put: There is evil in the world. It is in the news. It is in our common experience. Popular periodicals even grapple with it. Quite apart from any precommitment to a specific theory of evil and how evil fits in to a larger interpretation of life, there is a virtual consensus that something is deeply wrong with our world, that things do not always seem to go as they should, and that much too often events happen that are utterly dreadful. It is in this broad sense that we say, "Evil exists."

Evil and Religious Belief

As people through the centuries have reflected on the meaning of life, they have had to come to grips with the persistent and pervasive presence of evil. It is not surprising, then, that every major religion addresses evil within its unique frame of reference.[15] For Buddhism, evil is inherent in human existence, making nonexistence (*nirvana*) the goal. For Hinduism, evil belongs to the world of illusion (*maya*) and cyclical rebirth (*samsara*) from which we must seek to find release. For Zoroastrianism, evil is an eternal cosmic principle that opposes the good.

In *The Sacred Canopy*, sociologist Peter Berger writes that one function of every religion is to provide a way of understanding life, of fitting the events of life into a meaningful pattern. He explains that religion imposes order and lawfulness on experiences that seem to be chaotic and destructive—most notably, the phenomena of suffering and death. Thus, religion imposes a *nomos*, or lawful explanation, on otherwise anomic features of existence. Berger is worth quoting on this point:

> The anomic phenomena must not only be lived through, they must also be explained—to wit, explained in terms of the nomos established in the

society in question. An explanation of these phenomena in terms of religious legitimations, of whatever degree of theoretical sophistication, may be called a theodicy. It is important to stress here particularly (although the same point has already been made generally with respect to religious legitimations) that such an explanation need not entail a complex theoretical system. The illiterate peasant who comments upon the death of a child by referring to the will of God is engaging in theodicy as much as the learned theologian who writes a treatise to demonstrate that the suffering of the innocent does not negate the conception of a God both all-good and all-powerful. All the same, it is possible to differentiate theodicies in terms of their degree of rationality, that is, the degree to which they entail a theory that coherently and consistently explains the phenomena in question in terms of an over-all view of the universe. Such a theory, of course, once it is socially established, may be refracted on different levels of sophistication throughout the society. Thus, the peasant, when he speaks about the will of God, may himself intend, however inarticulately, the majestic theodicy constructed by the theologian.[16]

So, what a religious system says about evil reveals a great deal about what it takes ultimate reality and humanity's relation to it to be. Hence, the credibility of a religion is closely linked to its ability to give its adherents categories for thinking about the presence of evil.

Although evil poses a challenge that every major religion must address, the challenge to Christianity is particularly formidable. There seems to be a serious tension between what Christian theology affirms about the unrivaled power, unlimited knowledge, and unrelenting love of God, on the one hand, and what it admits about evil in God's created order, on the other. Many persons think that the Christian God—if He really exists and is the source and guarantor of value—would not allow the world to be as it is. This is the crux of the issue for Christian belief; it has traditionally been known as the problem of evil. Throughout history, Christian theologians and philosophers have wrestled with this problem. Thoughtful and sensitive laity have also felt the need for at least a general explanation of how to relate God and evil. The conundrum seems unavoidable. After reviewing all the evils that haunt our contemporary consciousness, Lance Morrow raises this precise problem at the end of his *Time* magazine article.[17]

Some thinkers believe that unless Christian believers have an acceptable solution to the problem of evil, they have no right to hold their distinctive theological position or to ask others to adopt it.[18] Philosopher T. W. Settle argues that grappling with the problem of evil is a "prolegomenon to intellectually honest theology."[19] Thor Hall proposes that the ability or inability to generate an answer to the vexing problem of evil is the litmus test of the "reasonableness of theology." Hall says that Christian thinkers must "be capable of handling honestly the actualities of human existence (realities which we all know) while at the same time providing a framework for explicating responsibly the essential affirmations of the faith (affirmations which are given within the historical tradition)."[20]

The position that is put under direct pressure by the presence of evil is known as "theism." Theism maintains that there exists a Supreme Being who is omnipotent, omniscient, and perfectly good. William Rowe calls this position "restricted theism."[21] Theism as such is not itself living religion but forms what we might call the basic conceptual foundation for several living religions: Christianity, Judaism, and Islam. The total belief frameworks of these actual religions involve adding certain other significant religious beliefs to restricted theism. Restricted theism conjoined with other religious claims constitutes what Rowe calls "expanded theism."

The present study treats many of the important discussions related to the basic theistic foundation of Christian belief (i.e., restricted theism). After all, insofar as evil presents a challenge to theism, it presents a challenge to any version of expanded theism. However, this study also considers some issues related to larger sets of Christian beliefs (i.e., various Christian versions of expanded theism). These sets of Christian beliefs particularly come into play when considering various responses to the challenge posed by evil. These larger sets of Christian beliefs are constituted, of course, by restricted theism conjoined with additional propositions about God's general purposes in the world, the role of Jesus Christ, life after death, the human condition, sin, and so forth. The specific propositions with which restricted theism is augmented—drawn from such sources as church creeds, biblical interpretation, and common Christian experience—determine the exact version of expanded theism at issue. Although we may refer to any one of these versions as "Christianity" or "Christian belief" or "Christian theology," we will more regularly use the more precise rubric "Christian theism."

The Philosophical Difficulty

Let us say that the essential problem here for theism (and thus for any version of Christian theism) is that of reconciling belief in an all-powerful, all-knowing, all-good deity with the belief that there is evil in the world. But exactly what kind of a problem is this? Speaking more precisely, the difficulty for theism lies in rebutting an argument that alleges some kind of conflict between beliefs about God and beliefs about evil. An argument from evil—or, really, any one of several arguments from evil—has a structure, premises, and conclusion. It is actually the conclusion of any given argument from evil and the reasons for that conclusion that are a "problem" for theism. In the following pages, I will use the term *problem of evil* simply as a synonym for *argument from evil*.[22] And there is not just one problem or argument from evil; there are actually many different arguments. Scholars have identified several major types of arguments from evil, noting their key strategies as well as characteristic theistic responses.

These arguments have various roots. For one thing, the problem of evil expresses a kind of moral protest and so involves categories of good and evil. For another thing, the problem involves religious beliefs about the existence and nature of God, giving it a distinct theological aspect. Yet the problem of evil is best understood as a philosophical problem. In its traditional role, philosophy clarifies and analyzes our beliefs, examines them for logical consistency and coherence, and evaluates their adequacy for explaining important human phenomena. These philosophical features make the discipline of philosophy the natural home field for the problem of evil.

There are, of course, many areas of philosophical concern, and each is determined by the exact set of ideas and issues that are examined: philosophy of science, philosophy of mind, philosophy of language, philosophy of art, and so forth. Each of these areas seeks to bring the key insights and interests of philosophy to bear upon the relevant topics. This means that typical philosophical questions about reality (metaphysics), knowledge (epistemology), and value (moral theory and axiology) are appropriate. And questions about the structure and acceptability of relevant arguments (logic) are always in order. The subject at hand, the problem of evil, falls within what is traditionally known as the philosophy of religion. It is the task of philosophy of religion, then, to bring these characteristic questions to bear on significant religious concepts and beliefs, such as those related to God, miracle, prayer, and faith.

Philosophers of religion have always been deeply interested in the question of whether there are rational grounds for either belief in God or disbelief in God. Impressive arguments have been constructed to show that God exists—such as the ontological, cosmological, and teleological arguments.[23] Likewise, a number of serious arguments have been advanced to show that God does not exist. Among those arguments against God's existence, none has been more prominent than the problem of evil. In the experience of evil and reflection upon it, humanity reaches the extreme limit—confronting the decisive question of the meaning of life, of the sense and nonsense of reality. Hans Küng states that the problem of evil is "the rock of atheism"[24] because so many people believe it to be intractable. This accounts for the lively and ongoing discussion of the problem in philosophy of religion.

But why, one might ask, should this philosophical problem be relevant to faith? Faith is personal commitment, deep abiding trust, firm conviction. Faith is much more than abstract reasoning. Why should the intricate arguments and counterarguments of philosophers affect religious faith at all? A sensible answer, it would seem, runs along the following lines. Although, granted, faith is *more* than mere intellectual assent to a set of beliefs, it is *at least* intellectual assent. Although faith is a personal trust in God, that trust is based on a number of important *beliefs* about what God is like and how persons may have a relationship to him. These beliefs are subject to philosophical scrutiny, critique, and defense. Thus, there really is no responsible way to insulate religious faith from philosophical reflection. And there is certainly no way to insulate it from the philosophical problem of evil.

The Classification of Evil

Recognizing the problem of evil as a serious challenge to Christian theism, it might seem advisable to begin our investigation with a precise definition of evil. However, the attempt to offer a specific definition at this point frequently ladens the meaning of evil with preconceived ideas and thus hinders objective discussion. Some thinkers, for example, define "evil" in theological terms as "sin" and consider the problem only in this light, reducing all evils to spiritual rebellion against God and its consequences. Other thinkers define "evil" as "finitude" and then treat all evil—even human perversity—as the inevitable results of creaturely limitation. Definitions of "evil" could be proposed and debated indefinitely. Therefore, it is advisable for present purposes to leave open the question of definition and proceed with a broad, commonsense notion of evil evoked by the things we typically call "evil."

Regardless of how we define it, we are all aware of the existence and profusion of evil. It is entirely possible to identify a whole spectrum of events and experiences as "evil." The set of commonly recognized evils includes, at the very least, such things as extreme pain and suffering, physical deformities, psychological abnormalities, the prosperity of bad people, the demise of good people, disrupted social relations, unfulfilled potential, a host of character defects, and natural catastrophes. This list specifies the sorts of things that are commonly considered evil without prejudicing later discussions. In philosophical parlance, this list indicates the *extension* of the term "evil" (i.e., all things to which the term applies) without specifying its exact *intension* (i.e., all that the term implies). The eloquent eighteenth-century skeptic David Hume followed this approach when he listed a sampling of the world's ills: "a hospital full of diseases, a prison crowded with malefactors and debtors, a field of battle strewed with carcasses, a fleet foundering in the ocean, a nation languishing under tyranny, famine, [and] pestilence."[25]

Evil indeed has many faces, faces with which we are all too familiar. Since the wide range of evils can be very confusing, most philosophers make a helpful distinction between *moral evil* and *natural evil.* In marking out the difference between the two broad kinds of evil, Alvin Plantinga writes that "we must distinguish between *moral evil* and *natural evil.* The former is evil which results from free human activity; natural evil is any other kind of evil."[26] As Plantinga admits, the distinction is not very precise. Yet this same point is made by John Hick: "Moral evil is evil what we human beings originate: cruel, unjust, vicious, and perverse thoughts and deeds. Natural evil is the evil that originates independently of human actions: in disease bacilli, earthquakes, storms, droughts, tornadoes, etc."[27]

Edward Madden and Peter Hare provide a similar classification:

> *Physical evil,* we shall say, denotes the terrible pain, suffering, and untimely death caused by events like fire, flood, landslide, hurricane, earthquake, tidal wave, and famine and by diseases like cancer, leprosy, and tetanus—as well as the crippling defects and deformities like blindness, deafness, dumbness, shriveled limbs, and insanity by which so many sentient beings are cheated of the full benefits of life. . . . *Moral evil* . . . denotes both moral wrong-doing such as lying, cheating, stealing, torturing, and murdering and character defects like greed, deceit, cruelty, wantonness, cowardice, and selfishness.[28]

Other authors do not depart far from this same general approach.

Although we could debate the exact boundaries between natural and moral evil, the basic distinction performs a helpful classificatory

function. It not only helps clarify our thinking about evil but also allows us to divide the general problem of evil into subsidiary problems
related to moral and to natural evil and thus guides further stages of
inquiry. In his penetrating treatment of the problem of evil, David
Hume shows he is aware of this important distinction. Hume observes that, in nature, "the stronger prey upon the weaker" and "the
weaker, too, in their turn, often prey upon the stronger, and vex and
molest them without relaxation." Acknowledging that humanity can
organize into societies and thus avoid some of the harm nature might
do, he insists that humans morally mistreat each other: "Oppression,
injustice, contempt, . . . violence, sedition, war, . . . treachery, fraud—
by these they mutually torment each other, and they would soon dis-
solve that society which they had formed were it not for the dread of
still greater ills which must attend their separation."[29]

Quite apart from technical philosophy, the distinction between natural and moral evil runs through most great literature. "The Tyger"
by William Blake is a powerful poetic expression of the problem of
natural evil. The poem forcefully raises the issue of whether a certain
instance of natural evil (e.g., the threat of being attacked by stronger
animals) could have been created by the God of the Christian faith.

> *Tyger! Tyger! burning bright*
> *In the forests of the night,*
> *What immortal hand or eye*
> *Could frame thy fearful symmetry?*
>
> *In what distant deeps or skies*
> *Burned the fire of thine eyes?*
> *On what wings dare he aspire?*
> *What the hand dare seize the fire?*
>
> *And what shoulder, and what art,*
> *Could twist the sinews of thy heart?*
> *And when thy heart began to beat,*
> *What dread hand? and what dread feet?*
>
> *What the hammer? what the chain?*
> *In what furnace was thy brain?*
> *What the anvil? what dread grasp*
> *Dare its deadly terrors clasp?*

When the stars threw down their spears,
And watered heaven with their tears,
Did he smile his work to see?
Did he who made the Lamb make Thee?

Tyger! Tyger! burning bright
In the forests of the night,
What immortal hand or eye
Dare frame thy fearful symmetry?[30]

We also find the problem of moral evil in great novels. Dostoevsky's classic *The Brothers Karamazov* contains a poignant treatment of the problem. Ivan Karamazov asks his brother Alyosha, who is a Russian Orthodox monk, the piercing question of why God allows cruelty to innocent children. Ivan relentlessly enumerates stories of the torture and murder of children—a little girl beaten by parents and then left overnight in an outhouse to freeze, a young serf boy torn to death by a landowner's hounds for throwing a stone at one of them, an unborn child cut from its mother's womb by invading Turks, and on and on. Then, Ivan cries: "Listen! I took the case of children only to make my case clearer. Of the other tears of humanity with which the earth is soaked from its crust to its center, I will say nothing. I have narrowed my subject on purpose. I am a bug, and I recognize in all humility that I cannot understand why the world is arranged as it is. . . . But then there are the children, and what am I to do about them? That's a question I can't answer."[31]

In the next six chapters, I explore the major atheistic arguments from evil as well as important theistic responses. I discuss the strengths and weaknesses on both sides and point directions for further discussion. In the process, I will not only analyze many technical issues related to God and evil but also attempt to develop a sense of the deep significance of this issue in human life. I address three problems of evil that express various logical and epistemological concerns: the logical problem, probabilistic problem, and evidential problem. The theistic responses to the logical and probabilistic problems that I examine can be described as defensive. The typical theistic response to the evidential problem that I inspect comes under the rubric of theodicy. I also explore what can be called the existential problem of evil, which expresses the intensely personal and moral aspects of the issue.

Notes

1. Lance Morrow, "Evil," *Time,* June 10, 1991, pp. 48–53.

2. The use of the masculine gender pronoun here does not imply that God is male. Historical Judeo-Christian views of God have affirmed that sexuality is a creaturely reality not reflected in God. My use of masculine gender pronouns when referring to God throughout this book, then, follows the tradition that requires us to use imperfect earthly terms and images to talk about God. I avoid using any new, revised God-language here, which would raise some very interesting but also very sophisticated controversies. I retain traditional usage simply for the sake of economy and getting on with the issues at hand.

3. Ron Rosenbaum, "Staring into the Heart of the Heart of Darkness," *New York Times Magazine* (June 4, 1995): 36–44, 50–58, 61, 72.

4. Fyodor Dostoevsky, *The Brothers Karamazov,* trans. Constance Garnett (New York: Norton, 1976), p. 97.

5. Robert Louis Stevenson, *The Strange Case of Dr. Jekyll and Mr. Hyde* (London: Folio Society, 1948), p. 124.

6. Ibid., p. 127.

7. Ibid., p. 146.

8. Ibid., pp. 124–125.

9. Rom. 7:15, 18b–19 New Revised Standard Version. Paul's lamentation should be read in context: See Rom. 7:15–20.

10. Augustine, *Confessions,* 8.5.10.

11. Herman Melville, *Moby Dick,* eds. H. Hayford and H. Parker (New York: W. W. Norton, 1967). For a discussion of this vision of life, see Henry A. Myers, *Tragedy: A View of Life* (Ithaca: Cornell University Press, 1956), pp. 57–77, and Richard Sewall, *The Vision of Tragedy* (New Haven: Yale University, 1959), pp. 92–105.

12. Ludwig Wittgenstein, *Tractatus Logico-Philosophicus,* trans. D. F. Pears and B. F. McGuinness (London: Routledge & Kegan Paul, 1971), proposition 6.4311, p. 147.

13. H. F. Lovell Cocks, *By Faith Alone* (London: James Clarke, 1943), p. 55.

14. T. S. Eliot, *Murder in the Cathedral: The Complete Poems* (New York: Harcourt, Brace, 1952), p. 180.

15. Such matters are discussed in John Bowker, *Problems of Suffering in Religions of the World* (Cambridge: Cambridge University Press, 1970).

16. Peter Berger, *The Sacred Canopy* (New York: Doubleday, 1967), pp. 53–54.

17. Morrow, "Evil," p. 51.

18. In response, some Christians hold that believers may instead argue that they do not need a theodicy. A number of approaches are possible here. For example, a believer may argue that since the problem of evil does not conclusively disprove her position, she need not answer it. Or a believer may argue that she has convincing proof of God's existence on other grounds

and hence that she knows the problem of evil must have some answer. She may even say that her belief in God is so basic that it supersedes efforts to prove or disprove it. This line of thought is discussed in Chapter 4.

However, it is fair to say that there are differing opinions about whether any way of avoiding the problem of evil can be comfortably accepted. After all, Christian theism purports to explain relevant features of human existence, but evil does not seem to fit well into the explanation. Therefore, there is at least a prima facie case that the Christian theist must make good her claim by addressing the problem of evil.

19. T. W. Settle, "A Prolegomenon to Intellectually Honest Theology," *Philosophical Forum* 1 (1978): 136–140.

20. Thor Hall, "Theodicy as a Test of the Reasonableness of Theology," *Religion in Life* 43 (1974): 204.

21. William Rowe, "Evil and the Theistic Hypothesis: A Response to Wykstra," *International Journal for Philosophy of Religion* 16 (1984): 95.

22. Daniel Howard-Snyder distinguishes between the "problem of evil" and the "argument from evil" in his edited volume *The Evidential Argument from Evil* (Bloomington: Indiana University Press, 1996), pp. XI-XII.

23. For a discussion of most of the major issues related to whether there are rational grounds for believing in God, see Michael Peterson, William Hasker, Bruce Reichenbach, and David Basinger, *Reason and Religious Belief: Introduction to the Philosophy of Religion*, 2nd ed. (New York: Oxford University Press, 1998).

24. Hans Küng, *On Being a Christian*, trans. Edward Quinn (Garden City, N.Y.: Doubleday, 1976), p. 432.

25. David Hume, *Dialogues Concerning Natural Religion*, cited in Michael L. Peterson, ed., *The Problem of Evil: Selected Readings* (Notre Dame, Ind.: University of Notre Dame Press, 1992), p. 42.

26. Alvin Plantinga, *God, Freedom, and Evil* (Grand Rapids, Mich.: Eerdmans, 1977), p. 30.

27. John Hick, *Evil and the God of Love*, rev. ed. (New York: Harper & Row, 1975), p. 12.

28. Edward Madden and Peter Hare, *Evil and the Concept of God* (Springfield, Ill.: Charles C. Thomas, 1968), p. 6.

29. Hume quoted in Peterson, ed., *The Problem of Evil*, p. 41.

30. William Blake, "The Tyger," in *The Portable Blake*, ed. Alfred Kazin (New York: Viking Press, 1968), p. 109.

31. Dostoevsky, *The Brothers Karamazov*, pp. 224–225.

Suggested Readings

Camus, Albert. *The Plague*. Translated by Stuart Gilbert. New York: Alfred A. Knopf, 1948.

Davis, Stephen T. "Why Did This Happen to Me?—The Patient as a Philosopher." *Princeton Seminary Bulletin* 65 (1972): 61–67.

Hick, John. "The Problem of Evil." In *The Encyclopedia of Philosophy.* Edited by Paul Edwards. New York: Macmillan and Free Press, 1967, pp. 136–141.

Hume, David. *Dialogues Concerning Natural Religion.* Parts 10 and 11. Edited by H. D. Aiken. New York: Hafner Publishing, 1955.

Lewis, C. S. *The Problem of Pain.* New York: Macmillan, 1962.

MacLeish, Archibald. *J. B.* Boston: Houghton Mifflin, 1986.

Melville, Herman. *Moby-Dick.* Edited by H. Hayford and Hershel Parker. New York: W. W. Norton, 1967.

Peterson, Michael L., ed. *The Problem of Evil: Selected Readings.* Notre Dame, Ind.: University of Notre Dame Press, 1992.

Pike, Nelson, ed. *God and Evil: Readings on the Theological Problem of Evil.* Englewood Cliffs, N.J.: Prentice-Hall, 1964.

Wiesel, Elie. *Night.* Translated by Stella Rodway. New York: Bantam Books, 1960.

_____. *The Trial of God.* Translated by Marion Wiesel. New York: Schocken Books, 1979.

2

The Logical Problem of Evil

The problem of evil has both theoretical and existential dimensions. The theoretical problems deal with logical and epistemic relationships between propositions about God and evil. The existential dimension of the problem pertains to one's deeply personal response to evil and overall sense of the worth of human existence. Leaving discussion of the existential problem until Chapter 7, I devote the intervening chapters to three important statements of the theoretical problem. During the 1970s and 1980s, philosophers came to make a distinction between two broad versions of the theoretical problem. The logical problem revolves around the question of consistency among key theistic propositions. The evidential problem involves evaluating propositions about God in terms of the facts of evil. I discuss two ways of advancing the evidential problem in Chapters 4 and 5. Here I focus on the classic logical problem of evil.

Statement of the Problem

The logical problem of evil (also called the a priori problem and the deductive problem) arises on the basis of an alleged inconsistency between certain claims about God and certain claims about evil.[1] Historically, the discussion of this problem has developed as critics attempt to expose an inconsistency among theistic beliefs and theistic philosophers attempt to show why there is no inconsistency.

Oxford philosopher J. L. Mackie sums up the atheistic challenge: "Here it can be shown, not that religious beliefs lack rational support, but that they are positively irrational, that several parts of the essential

theological doctrine are inconsistent with one another."[2] Since being
logically consistent is necessary for a set of beliefs to be rational,
Mackie's charge is very serious. Mackie clearly and forcefully states
the logical problem: "In its simplest form the problem is this: God is
omnipotent; God is wholly good; and yet evil exists. There seems to
be some contradiction between these three propositions, so that if
any two of them were true the third would be false. But at the same
time all three are essential parts of most theological positions; the theologian, it seems, at once *must* adhere and *cannot consistently* adhere
to all three."[3]

If Mackie and other critics are right, then the dilemma facing the
theist is whether to retain his theistic position and the propositions
that constitute it (and thus be saddled with a contradiction) or to relinquish one or more of the relevant propositions (and thereby escape
the contradiction). To embrace a contradiction is irrational, but to
surrender any key theistic belief is to abandon standard theism.

Two centuries ago, David Hume (following Epicurus) posed the
difficulty with stark clarity: "Is [God] willing to prevent evil, but not
able? Then he is impotent. Is he able, but not willing? Then he is
malevolent. Is he both able and willing? Whence then is evil?"[4] Or
consider H. J. McCloskey's succinct statement: "The problem of evil
is a very simple one to state. There is evil in the world; yet the world
is said to be the creation of a good and omnipotent God. How is this
possible? Surely a good omnipotent God would have made a world
free of evil of any kind."[5] Similar expressions of the logical problem
are abundant in the philosophical literature.

If we isolate for closer inspection the propositions that critics commonly have in mind, we get the following list of propositions:

(1) God exists;
(2) God is all-powerful;
(3) God is all-good;
(4) God is all-knowing;
(5) Evil exists.

The set of beliefs (1)–(4) is what Rowe calls "restricted theism," a position that the theist, by virtue of being a theist, must accept. However, the typical theist also accepts (5) as an element in his overall position. The critic, then, maintains that the set (1)–(5) is logically
inconsistent.

The Structure and Strategy of the Argument

Before embarking on a complete discussion of the logical argument from evil, it is helpful to review the general concept of *inconsistency* or *contradiction*.[6] Actually, there are several types of contradiction to consider. One type is a certain kind of proposition—a conjunctive proposition in which one conjunct is the denial or negation of the other conjunct. Consider the following proposition:

(6) Socrates is mortal, and it is false that Socrates is mortal.

The first conjunct (Socrates is mortal) and the second conjunct (it is false that Socrates is mortal) cannot both be true. What we have here is an *explicit contradiction*.

The problem, of course, is that one who asserts a contradiction cannot be advancing a position that is completely true. By methods found in any elementary text on logic, we can know that a contradiction is a proposition that is necessarily false. Interestingly, knowing the actual truth or falsity of the conjuncts in a contradictory proposition is not required in order to know that it suffers from inconsistency. Presumably, few people commit such flagrant errors in thinking.

Mackie speaks of a *set* of theistic propositions being inconsistent or containing a contradiction. But what does it mean for a set to be inconsistent or contradictory? We may say that a set of propositions is explicitly contradictory if one of the members is the denial or negation of another member. For example, consider the following set:

(7) Socrates is mortal
(8) It is false that Socrates is mortal.

By conjoining these two propositions, we get the familiar contradiction (6). A set from which such a contradiction can be generated is explicitly contradictory in the sense in question.

In many cases, however, a set of propositions is contradictory but the contradiction is not obvious, not explicit. In these more difficult instances, the charge of inconsistency can still be made to stick if ordinary rules of formal logic can be used to deduce a contradiction.[7] Let us develop an example to show how this works. Call the following set *A*:

(9)   If all men are mortal, then Socrates is mortal
(10) All men are mortal
(8)   It is false that Socrates is mortal.

Using the logical rule *modus ponens* (if *p*, then *q*; *p*; therefore *q*), we can deduce

(7) Socrates is mortal

from (9) and (10). Proposition (7) is logically inconsistent with (8). Since it is not possible for propositions (7) and (8) both to be true at the same time; the set from which they are drawn is contradictory. We shall say that set *A* is *formally contradictory* because we can deduce an explicit contradiction from its member propositions by the laws of formal logic.

Admittedly, this example of an inconsistent set of propositions is a simplified one; seldom do such easy cases occur in ordinary life. In fact, the propositions that form an inconsistency in an opponent's position are sometimes not stated at all. So, the critic is faced with the double task of first producing all of the relevant unstated propositions and then drawing out the contradiction from the fully articulated position. In such cases, the sets of propositions in question are *implicitly contradictory*.

For a third example, let us reflect on the following propositions as forming an implicitly contradictory set:

(11) Socrates is older than Plato
(12) Plato is older than Aristotle
(13) Socrates is not older than Aristotle.

This set—which I will designate *B*—is not explicitly contradictory; it is also not formally contradictory. We cannot use the laws of logic to deduce the denial of any of these propositions from the others. Yet there is an important sense in which set *B* is inconsistent or contradictory. That is, it is *not possible* that its three members are all true.

Now, it is *necessarily true* that

(14) If Socrates is older than Plato, and Plato is older than Aristotle, then Socrates is older than Aristotle.

If we add (14) to *B*, we get a set that is formally contradictory. Employing the laws of formal logic, (11), (12), and (14) yield the denial of (13). Now we have succeeded in making the implicit contradiction explicit.

We were able to deduce the contradiction in this set because we employed an additional proposition that is *necessarily true*. There are actually different varieties of necessary truth. The truth of some propositions—such as (15) below—can be established by the laws of logic alone.

(15)   If all men are mortal and Socrates is a man, then Socrates is mortal.

This expresses a truth of logic. Yet the truths of arithmetic and mathematics generally are also necessarily true, such as

(16) 2 + 2 = 4.

Furthermore, there are many propositions that are neither truths of logic nor truths of mathematics but are nonetheless necessarily true, such as (14). A few more examples of this type of necessary truth would be

(17) Bachelors are unmarried males
(18) Blue is a color
(19) No numbers are horses.

Let us call the type of necessity with which we are dealing here *broadly logical necessity*. There is a correlative kind of possibility as well: A proposition *p* is possibly true (in the broadly logical sense) just in case its negation or denial is not necessarily true (in that same broadly logical sense).

Necessity and possibility in the broadly logical sense must be distinguished from another sense of necessity and possibility. That other sense is *causal* or *natural* necessity and possibility. For instance,

(20) Michael Jordan has leapt over the Sears Tower.

is a proposition that is possibly true in our sense of broadly logical possibility. Yet in the sense of causal or natural possibility, it is not possible at all. Human beings—even great athletes—just do not have the physical endowments required for such a feat. There are a number of propositions, furthermore, about which it is difficult to say whether they are or are not possible in the broadly logical sense, thus giving rise to philosophical controversy. For example, is it possible for a person to exist in a disembodied state?

Without attempting to settle the more subtle philosophical problems lurking in this area, we now are in a good position to define what it means for a set of propositions to be *implicitly contradictory*. A set *S* of propositions is implicitly contradictory if there is a necessary proposition *p* such that the conjunction of *p* with *S* is a formally contradictory set. Alternatively, we might say: *S* is implicitly contradictory if there is some necessarily true proposition *p* such that by using just the laws of logic, we can deduce an explicit contradiction from *p* together with the members of *S*.

Now that we have defined the concept of implicit contradiction, we are in a position to understand how Mackie frames up the logical argument from evil. His atheistic challenge is essentially that theism is a system of inconsistent beliefs—that is, that a contradiction can be derived from central theistic propositions about God and evil. However, the contradiction is not an explicit one. In addition, it does not appear that a formal contradiction can be deduced from basic theistic propositions. So, Mackie and other critics who make this argument are faced with the task of supplementing the basic propositions of theism with one or more necessary truths in order to deduce the fatal contradiction. In fact, Mackie's strategy is to specify additional propositions that relate to the meanings of key terms used in the original set of theistic propositions:

> The contradiction does not arise immediately; to show it we need some additional premises, or perhaps some quasi-logical rules connecting the terms "good," "evil," and "omnipotent." The additional principles are that good is opposed to evil, in such a way that a good thing always eliminates evil as far as it can, and that there are no limits to what an omnipotent thing can do. From these it follows that a good omnipotent thing eliminates evil completely, and then the propositions that a good omnipotent thing exists, and that evil exists, are incompatible.[8]

Here we have Mackie's way of generating the contradiction.

In the vigorous debate that surrounded the logical problem, critics typically used supplemental propositions from the following list:

(1') God is a real being independent from the world
(2') An omnipotent being can bring about any logically possible state of affairs
(3') A wholly good being is opposed to evil and tries to eliminate it as far as it can
(4') An omniscient being knows everything that it is logically possible to know
(5') The existence of evil is not logically necessary.

One can readily see how each proposition here defines or extends the meanings of central theistic claims. The atheistic critic maintains that propositions such as these, together with the original set of theistic propositions, generate a contradiction. Other supplemental propositions become relevant as we consider the several distinct versions of the logical problem.

Versions of the Logical Argument

The atheistic critic's basic strategy is to demonstrate how the essential theistic claims are implicitly contradictory. And these critics have not differed significantly over the set of theistic claims that contains the contradiction. As we saw above, the following set is frequently cited:

(1) God exists;
(2) God is omnipotent;
(3) God is omniscient;
(4) God is wholly good.
(5) Evil exists.

For brevity and clarity, let us abbreviate the theistic position expressed by propositions (1)–(4) in one complex proposition:

(G) An omnipotent, omniscient, wholly good God exists.

Any question about (G) is equivalent, then, to a question about one or more of the propositions that are incorporated into it. Our subsequent analysis will focus on the issue between those atheists who advance the charge of inconsistency and those theists who refuse to give up (G) or any of its constituent propositions in order to escape the charge. Such defenders qualify as true theists, whereas those who relinquish or modify (G) are actually quasi-theists[9] whom we shall discuss in Chapter 6.

Actually, there are three distinct versions of the logical problem of evil, with each version being determined by exactly which proposition about evil it employs. As we have seen, many critics (Hume, Mackie, McCloskey, and others) take the belief in the existence of evil—expressed in proposition (5) above—to form an inconsistent set when conjoined with set (1)–(4). And clearly, this formulation of the problem has been the most widely discussed. However, other critics do not believe that the inconsistency arises when some proposition about the sheer existence of evil is added to the set of propositions (1)–(4). Instead, they hold that the more important logical problem of evil is formed by adding to (1)–(4) some proposition about the great extent and profusion of evil. Plantinga recognizes that this second formulation of the problem is open to the critic who would say that "God's existence is not consistent with the vast *amount* and *variety* of moral evil the universe actually contains."[10] A third version of the logical problem, a version that does not focus either on the sheer existence of evil or on its profusion, has been raised by a few critics. Terence Penelhum, for example, insists that "it is logically inconsistent for a theist to admit the existence of a pointless evil."[11] The critic raising this version of the logical argument assumes that the theist believes both that God exists and that pointless evil exists.

We may now distinguish three versions of the logical argument from evil, depending on which problematic belief about evil the critic attributes to theism. The critic can formulate an argument to the effect that (G) is inconsistent with any *one* of the three propositions below:

(E_1) Evil exists;
(E_2) Large amounts, extreme kinds, and perplexing distributions of evil exist;
(E_3) Gratuitous or pointless evil exists.

When conjoined with (G), each of the preceding propositions determines a different formulation or version of the logical problem.

Let us develop a helpful taxonomy of the logical problem, as presented in Figure 2.1. All three versions of this argument here are exactly the same in having a purely deductive structure and a strategy of deriving an implicit contradiction.

FIGURE 2.1   Versions of the Logical Argument from Evil

I	*II*	*III*
(G) is inconsistent with (E_1)	(G) is inconsistent with (E_2)	(G) is inconsistent with (E_3)

Since Version I is clearly the most influential and most widely discussed formulation, we shall treat it as the paradigmatic version of the logical problem of evil and give it close attention. Besides, most of the analysis of Version I applies mutatis mutandis to Versions II and III.

The essence of Version I is that the theist believes in the existence and relevant perfections of God, on the one hand, and that there is evil, on the other. The atheistic critic understands this set of beliefs to be implicitly contradictory. Casting the difficulty in terms of the precise propositions involved, we have the following logical situation. The theist is officially committed to

(G) An omnipotent, omniscient, wholly good God exists

as well as to

(E_1) Evil exists.

However, it appears to the atheistic critic that proposition (G), when supplemented by the appropriate necessary propositions, entails

($\sim E_1$) Evil does not exist.

Now if (G) does entail ($\sim E_1$), then the theist is unwittingly committed to both (E_1) and ($\sim E_1$). This means that his beliefs are inconsistent because both (E_1) and ($\sim E_1$) figure into his theological position. In order to vindicate himself rationally, the theist must clarify and reconcile the propositions that supposedly generate the contradiction.

It is commonly agreed that the alleged contradiction is not immediately forthcoming from propositions (G) and (E_1). So, the critic must invoke the strategy previously explained for exposing implicit contradictions—that is, she must add certain propositions to (G) and

(E_1). Let us review a representative selection of auxiliary propositions often cited by the atheistic critic:

(1.1)   God is a real being transcendent from the world
(2.1)   God can bring about any logically possible state of affairs, including the elimination of evil
(3.1)   God knows everything that it is possible to know, including how to eliminate evil
(4.1)   God always seeks to promote good and eliminate evil
(5.1)   The existence of evil is not a logically necessary state of affairs.

Now, from (G), together with (1.1)–(5.1), it follows that

(~E1) Evil does not exist,

a conclusion that clearly contradicts (E_1). At this point, the atheist seems to have made good her charge of inconsistency by deriving from the theist's position two logically incompatible propositions: (E_1) and (~E1). Obviously, by the law of noncontradiction, these two propositions cannot both be true at the same time and in the same sense. Hence, anyone holding both propositions is irrational.

The reasoning behind this indictment is not hard to grasp and resembles the third example above, in which unstated belief (14) had to be supplied in order to set up the contradiction. Theists say that God exists and has a definite character. It is natural to presume that God's character can be used as a basis for explaining (and perhaps predicting) his actions, even actions related to evil in the world. For present purposes, this means that the terms in proposition (G) have specifiable meanings that can be delineated in additional propositions such as (1.1)–(4.1). Furthermore, there is no logical necessity that evil exist, as indicated by (5.1). From (G) together with (1.1)–(5.1), it is a fairly elementary exercise in deductive logic to derive

(~E_1) Evil does not exist.

Yet evil does exist, and its existence is recognized by the typical theist:

(E_1)   Evil exists.

The classical logical problem as represented by Version I is thus forged. This is the kind of case that Mackie and many other atheistic critics articulate.

Other propositions would have to be stated in order to forge Versions II and III. For instance, a proposition much like the following would be needed in Version II:

(4.2) God's goodness would seek to prevent or eliminate large amounts, extreme kinds, and perplexing distributions of evil.

Something like

(4.3) God's goodness would not allow gratuitous or pointless evil to exist.

would be needed to articulate fully Version III. But we need not pursue discussion of these versions here. The strategy is the same for all versions of the logical problem of evil. The atheistic critic derives a contradiction from a set of propositions that the theist allegedly accepts. How shall the theist respond?

The Burden of Proof

In assessing the state of the debate between the theist and the atheistic critic, it is helpful to review how the logical problem of evil develops. The theist holds a set of beliefs, and the critic claims that they are inconsistent. This places the initial burden on the critic to state the inconsistency, to draw it out, to make it obvious. The critic's strategy, then, is to attempt to generate a contradiction from a designated set of the theist's own beliefs. Otherwise, it would not be possible to make the accusation that the theist's beliefs are inconsistent stick. Once the critic has made the opening foray, the theist must respond by showing what is wrong with the critic's case.

Consider Version I of the logical problem of evil, which we have chosen as a model. Here the critic maintains that the theist holds contradictory beliefs, (G) and (E_1). In order to bring this contradiction to light, the critic must show that (G) ultimately entails ($\sim E_1$). If the critic can do this, she will thereby show that the theist's position involves both (E_1) and ($\sim E_1$), the belief that evil exists as well as the belief that evil does not exist. This is a plain contradiction. For Version II, the critic's strategy would be similar. She would need to deduce two propositions from theistic commitments: one stating that there are amounts, kinds, and distributions of evil that God would not allow and one indicating that those amounts, kinds, and distributions exist. This would constitute a contradiction. For Version III, the required atheistic strategy is now quite familiar. It must be proved that the theist is committed to the belief that God would not allow gratuitous evil *and* to the belief that gratuitous evil exists—again, two contradictory beliefs.

The significance of the charge of logical inconsistency is not difficult to comprehend. Two propositions that are inconsistent cannot both be true at the same time and in the same sense, such as

(21) Kant is a great philosopher

and

(22) It is not the case that Kant is a great philosopher.

Any position involving such a contradiction, then, cannot be wholly true. In the issue over God and evil, the critic declares that it is not possible for both (G) and some (E)-like proposition to be true and yet that, on some grounds or other, the theist is committed to both.

Although the burden of deducing a contradiction from theistic beliefs rests squarely on the shoulders of the atheistic critic, Alvin Plantinga has correctly stated the conditions that any critic must meet: "To make good his claim the atheologian must provide some proposition which is either necessarily true, or essential to theism, or a logical consequences of such propositions."[12] Clearly, there is no logical problem for the theist if he is not committed to each proposition in the set or if the set does not really entail a contradiction. If the critic uses an additional proposition that is necessarily true, then the theist must accept it because it must be accepted by all rational people. If the additional proposition is essential to any theistic position, then the theist must accept it by virtue of being a theist. And of course, the theist must accept any logical consequence of his propositions as well.

The critic's aim is to show that it is not possible that both (G) and (E_1) be true. If she can come up with an additional proposition—or

set of propositions—that the theist must accept and derive a contradiction from it together with the other relevant theistic propositions,
the theist is in serious trouble. Theistic defenders, such as Plantinga,
maintain that it is enormously difficult to come up with a proposition
that meets the conditions of being necessarily true, essential to theism, or a logical consequence of such propositions. On these grounds
alone, theists may argue that it is far from clear that it is not possible
for both (G) and (E$_1$) to be true.

Extending the theistic response further, Plantinga pioneered a
method for showing that it is possible for both (G) and (E$_1$) to be
true—a method that can presumably be used against the charge of inconsistency aimed at (G) and any (E)-like proposition. Succeeding at
this task is equivalent to denying the claim made by Mackie and others that it is not possible for both (G) and (E$_1$) to be true. According
to Plantinga, the theist need not show that both propositions are in
fact true in order to rebut the critic's charge. Rebutting the charge of
inconsistency relies on making some fine distinctions in the meanings
of key theistic terms (e.g., omnipotence) and then on supplying additional propositions that reflect a possible understanding of a theistic
worldview. These maneuvers directly challenge the critic's auxiliary
definitions and thus block her ability to deduce a contradiction from
theistic beliefs.

In Chapter 3, I embark on a full-scale discussion of what Plantinga
and other theists have done to defend against Version I of the logical
problem of evil. I particularly focus on a contemporary theistic response known as the Free Will Defense, which has already become classic. However, I will first briefly rehearse some of the basic moves that
theists can make to defend against Versions II and III, although these
versions, unlike Version I, have not attracted widespread interest.

In addressing the challenge posed by Version II, theists have main-
tained that critics have not successfully shown belief in God to imply
that he would limit the evil in the world to manageable amounts,
kinds, and distributions. Theists can construe divine goodness,
power, and knowledge as able to allow very large amounts, extreme
kinds, and perplexing distributions of evil. God might do this for a
number of different reasons: for example, to preserve a wide range of
free human choices or to allow the regular operation of impersonal
natural objects. Theists taking this line in effect argue that they need
not accept some of the additional propositions that critics use to deduce a contradiction from key theistic beliefs. So, it is not clear that

critics can establish that theists hold beliefs that imply both that God limits the amounts, kinds, and distributions of evil and that those limits have been exceeded.

Theists who respond to Version III grapple with the charge that they are committed to the proposition that God would not allow gratuitous evil, as well as the proposition that gratuitous evil exists. The working assumption of the atheistic critic here is that theism recognizes the existence of very severe evils as long as they have some point or meaning. However, certain stock responses suffice to refute the critic's formulation for Version III. The theist can take a very traditional approach and argue that he is not really committed to (E_3)—that is, that he does not believe that gratuitous or pointless evils exist. He can argue that his position necessitates that all evils, no matter how severe, must be meaningful or justified. Many theists understand their position in precisely this way. The theist who has this orientation might even venture some explanation or range of explanations designed to cover particularly troublesome evils. Some theists, however, construe their position differently and actually accept (E_3). These theists must take a different tack, then, in defending against Version III of the logical problem. They can seek to point out that the additional assumptions that the critic employs to derive the contradiction—such as (4.3)—are neither essential to theism nor necessarily true. Since this line of discussion is very rare in the philosophical literature on the logical problem of evil, I will wait to analyze it fully until Chapter 5, where it surfaces in relation to the evidential problem.

We can now see that the issue before us turns on the ability of critics, on the one hand, to show that theists must accept all of the propositions they use to deduce a contradiction and on the ability of theists, on the other hand, to show that they need not accept all of them. The only appropriate grounds for insisting that theists must accept the propositions are that they are either necessarily true, essential to theism, or a consequence of such propositions. Having framed the debate in this manner, I must note that an impressive number of critics have been convinced that serious logical difficulties exist for theism, and they have labored vigorously to bring them to light. Likewise, there are a number of theists who have taken seriously the matter of logical inconsistency and have worked diligently to defend against such attacks. At present, there is a large consensus that theistic maneuvers have been very effective and that the burden still rests on the shoulders of the critic to produce the contradiction. In the next chapter, I will turn to the line of debate in the philosophical literature that is widely thought to support this sentiment.

Notes

1. The following works employ these different labels for the problem: William Rowe, *Philosophy of Religion: An Introduction* (Encino and Belmont, Calif.: Dickenson, 1978), pp. 80–86; Michael L. Peterson, "Christian Theism and the Problem of Evil," *Journal of the Evangelical Theological Society* 21 (1978): 35–46; and Alvin Plantinga, *God and Other Minds: A Study of the Rational Justification of Belief in God* (Ithaca: Cornell University Press, 1967), p. 128.

2. J. L. Mackie, "Evil and Omnipotence," *Mind* 64 (1955): 200.

3. Ibid.

4. David Hume, *Dialogues Concerning Natural Religion*, ed. Henry D. Aiken (New York: Hafner, 1948), p. 66.

5. H. J. McCloskey, "The Problem of Evil," *Journal of Bible and Religion* 30 (1962): 187.

6. I will follow Plantinga's discussion throughout this exposition. See his *God, Freedom, and Evil* (Grand Rapids, Mich.: Eerdmans, 1977), pp. 12–24.

7. Irving, M. Copi and Carl Cohen, *Introduction to Logic, 10th Edition* (Englewood Cliffs, N.J.: Prentice-Hall, 1998), pp. 342–391.

8. Mackie, "Evil and Omnipotence," p. 209.

9. This terminology is borrowed from Edward Madden and Peter Hare, *Evil and the Concept of God* (Springfield, Ill.: Charles C. Thomas, 1968), chap. 6, pp. 104–136.

10. Plantinga, *God, Freedom, and Evil*, p. 55. Also see remarks in his *The Nature of Necessity* (Oxford: Clarendon Press, 1974), pp. 190–191.

11. Terence Penelhum, "Divine Goodness and the Problem of Evil," in *Readings in the Philosophy of Religion: An Analytic Approach*, ed. Baruch Brody (Englewood Cliffs, N.J.: Prentice-Hall, 1974), p. 226.

12. Plantinga, *God and Other Minds*, p. 117.

Suggested Readings

Adams, Marilyn M., and Robert M. Adams. *The Problem of Evil.* New York: Oxford University Press, 1990.

Ahern, M. B. *The Problem of Evil.* New York: Schocken Books, 1971.

Feinberg, John S. *The Many Faces of Evil: Theological Systems and the Problem of Evil.* 2nd ed. Grand Rapids, Mich.: Zondervan, 1994.

Flew, Antony. "Divine Omnipotence and Human Freedom." *Hibbert Journal* 53 (January 1955): 135–144.

Gale, Richard. *On the Nature and Existence of God*. Cambridge: Cambridge University Press, 1991.

Mackie, J. L. "Evil and Omnipotence." *Mind* 64 (1955): 200.

_____. "The Problem of Evil." In *The Miracle of Theism*. Oxford: Clarendon Press, 1982.

McCloskey, H. J. *God and Evil*. The Hague: Martinus Nijhoff, 1974.

Peterson, Michael. "Evil and Inconsistency." *Sophia (Australia)* 18 (July 1979): 20–27.

Peterson, Michael L., ed. *The Problem of Evil: Selected Readings*. Notre Dame, Ind.: University of Notre Dame Press, 1992.

Peterson, Michael, William Hasker, Bruce Reichenbach, and David Basinger. *Reason and Religious Belief: An Introduction to the Philosophy of Religion*. 2nd ed. New York: Oxford University Press, 1998, chap. 6, pp. 116–145.

Plantinga, Alvin. *God and Other Minds: A Study of the Rational Justification of Belief in God*. Ithaca: Cornell University Press, 1967.

_____. *God, Freedom, and Evil*. Grand Rapids, Mich.: Eerdmans, 1977.

_____. *The Nature of Necessity*. Oxford: Clarendon Press, 1974.

_____. "Which Worlds Could God Have Created?" *Journal of Philosophy* 70 (1973): 539–552.

Reichenbach, Bruce. "The Deductive Argument from Evil." *Sophia (Australia)* 20 (April 1981): 25–42.

_____. *Evil and a Good God*. New York: Fordham University Press, 1982.

3

The Function of Defense

Just as we have classified the two major versions of the problem of evil into the *logical* and *evidential* formulations, we may also classify the two main responses to the problem as *defense* and *theodicy*. The aim of defense is to show that antitheistic arguments from evil—either logical or evidential—are not successful on their own terms. The general aim of theodicy, by contrast, is to give positive, plausible reasons for the existence of evil in a theistic universe. Defense has come to be the theistic strategy most closely associated with discussions of the logical formulation of the problem of evil, whereas theodicy has come to be associated with the evidential formulation. Much controversy has arisen over the relative need for defense and theodicy, and we shall later see how these differences play out in the literature on God and evil.

The Free Will Defense

The present task is to review and evaluate a very fascinating and instructive part of the debate over the logical problem. Taking Version I of the logical problem of evil as a point of departure, Alvin Plantinga developed a response that has now come to be known as the Free Will Defense. Plantinga's famous Free Will Defense was produced in both 1967 and 1974 renditions.[1] Since the later rendition exploits the most current and sophisticated ideas in formal logic, I will use it as the basis for the present discussion.

As we have seen, philosophers such as J. L. Mackie have charged that it is logically inconsistent for a theist to believe that

(G) An omnipotent, omniscient, wholly good God exists

and that

(E₁) Evil exists.

This accusation is tantamount to claiming that it is not possible for both propositions to be true together—that the conjunction of (G) and (E₁) is necessarily false. The critics' strategy is to try to produce a proposition that is at least plausibly thought to be necessarily true and whose conjunction with our original two propositions formally yields a contradiction. Defenders insist that critics have never produced a plausible candidate for this role.

   In fact, many theists through the centuries—perhaps inspired most notably by Augustine—have thought that the theme of free will provides a basis for rejecting the critics' charge that God and evil are incompatible. Although full discussion of St. Augustine's view of evil appears in Chapter 6, I must note here his emphasis on divinely created free will: "If man is a good, and cannot act rightly unless he wills to do so, then he must have free will, without which he can not act rightly. We must not believe that God gave us free will so that we might sin, just because sin is committed through free will."[2] The point is that our humanity is of great value and that free will is necessary to our humanity. Human beings have moral significance because we have the ability to make choices that are morally right or wrong. Yet God cannot give us the power to make morally right choices without giving us the power to make morally wrong ones as well. So, in order to have the good of humanity itself as well as the good choices that humanity might make, God must permit evil. Many theists through the centuries have found St. Augustine's reasoning on this matter very compelling.

   Alvin Plantinga is well known for applying this line of reasoning in a very specific manner to the precise way in which the charge of inconsistency was formulated. Against the logical problem, he crafts a defense. Unlike Augustine's discussion, which affirms the reality of creaturely free will, Plantinga's discussion turns on the pure logical possibility of such. As Plantinga recognizes, the success of the defense hinges on a certain understanding of what is meant by *a person's being free with respect to an action*. For the Free Will Defender, if a person is free with respect to an action, then he is free either to perform or to refrain from the action. No causal laws and antecedent conditions determine that he will perform or not perform the action. In other words, at the time in question, it is within the person's power to perform the action and within his power to refrain from performing the action. What it means for *a person to go wrong with respect to a morally significant action* is for it to be wrong for him to perform it and he does or wrong for him not to and he does not.

According to Plantinga, a preliminary statement of the Free Will Defense would go as follows: A world containing significantly free creatures (who can freely choose between good and evil) is more valuable, all other things being equal, than a world containing no free creatures whatsoever. God, of course, can create free creatures, but then he cannot *cause* or *determine* that they only perform right actions. Doing this would preempt their significant freedom. Hence, there is no way for God to create creatures capable of moral good without thereby creating creatures capable of moral evil. Conversely, God cannot eliminate the possibility of moral evil without eliminating the possibility of moral good. The fact, then, that some creatures have gone wrong in the exercise of their freedom since the dawn of creation does not count against God's omnipotence or goodness. Having gained a sense of this perspective, we may now state the central claim of the Free Will Defense: It is possible that God could not have created a universe containing moral good (or as much moral good as this one contains) without creating one containing moral evil.

The Compatibilist Position

Critics, of course, are not unfamiliar with the recurring theme of free will in much theistic thought. Antony Flew and J. L. Mackie raised a very important objection to the Free Will Defense that had to be met before the defense could be totally effective. The objection rests on the claim that it is logically possible that there could be a world containing significantly free beings who always do what is right. Since there is no contradiction or inconsistency in this claim, it means that there are possible worlds containing moral good but no moral evil. Since God is omnipotent—and thus can bring about any logically possible state of affairs—God must be able to create a world containing moral good but no moral evil. In other words, God might have made people so that they always freely do the right thing. As Flew expresses it, "If there is no contradiction here then Omnipotence might have made a world inhabited by wholly virtuous people."[3] If this is so, then, as Flew says, "the Free Will Defense is broken-backed," and "we are back again with the original intractable antinomy."[4]

Flew is not alone in voicing this line of reasoning. Mackie puts it forthrightly:

> If God has made men such that in their free choices they sometimes prefer what is good and sometimes what is evil, why could he not have made men such that they always freely choose the good? If there is no logical impossibility in a man's freely choosing the good on one, or on several occasions, there cannot be a logical impossibility in his freely choosing the good on every occasion. God was not, then, faced with a choice between making innocent automata and making beings who, in acting freely, would sometimes go wrong: there was open to him the obviously better possibility of making beings who would act freely but always go right. Clearly, his failure to avail himself of this possibility is inconsistent with his being both omnipotent and wholly good.[5]

The position championed here is known as *compatibilism*. It is the view that freedom and determinism—even divine determinism—are compatible.

Put another way, the compatibilists' point is that the proposition

(23) God brings it about that human beings always choose what is right

is logically consistent with the proposition

(24) human beings have free choice.

This position directly opposes the Free Will Defense, which, as we have already seen, relies on an *incompatibilist* position: the view that (23) and (24) are logically inconsistent.

As we would expect, the controversy between Free Will Defenders and critics historically revolved around the issue of how key concepts such as omnipotence and free will should be understood. Although the Free Will Defender may agree with critics that a world in which all persons freely choose to do what is right is indeed a possible world, he seeks to qualify our understandings of free will and omnipotence in a way that avoids the dilemma presented by the critic. Obviously, the critic here believes that an omnipotent deity can create just any logically possible world he selects. A wholly good deity would select the world that is best on the whole, a world that we would surely deem to be one in which everyone freely does what is right. At this point, we have come to the hotly contested claim that God could have created any possible world he pleased.[6] The defender counters that God, though omnipotent, could not have created just any possible world. At this point, we must pause to consider how Free Will Defenders have come to frame the issue of free will and omnipotence in terms of contemporary ideas about possible worlds.

The Incompatibilist Rejoinder

Since Plantinga is credited with first putting the Free Will Defense in terms of the logic of possible worlds, we will consider his vindication of incompatibilism.[7] We may say that a possible world is a way things could have been, a total possible state of affairs. Among states of affairs, some are actual, and some are not. For example, *the Kentucky Wildcats' being the "winningest" basketball team in NCAA history* is a state of affairs, as is *Abraham Lincoln's being the first president of the United States.* However, the former is actual, whereas the latter is not. Although the latter is not actual, it is still a possible state of affairs. Possible states of affairs must be distinguished from impossible ones, and impossible ones must be further distinguished. Both *Beth's having climbed Mt. Everest in five minutes flat* and *John's having squared the circle* are impossible states of affairs. The former is causally or naturally impossible; the latter is impossible in the broadly logical sense.

A possible world, then, is a possible state of affairs in the sense that it is possible in the broadly logical sense. Although a possible world is a state of affairs, not every state of affairs is a possible world. To have the status of a possible world, a state of affairs must be *complete* or *maximal.* *Socrates' having been executed by drinking hemlock* is a possible state of affairs, but it is not complete or inclusive enough to be a possible world. Completeness must now be defined. A state of affairs S *includes* state of affairs S' if is not possible that S obtain and S' fail to obtain. Likewise, the conjunctive state of affairs S *but not* S' is not possible. A state of affairs S *precludes* another state of affairs S' if it is not possible that *both* obtain. In other words, S precludes S' if the conjunctive state of affairs S *and* S' is impossible. Now, a complete or maximal state of affairs—that is, a possible world—is one that either includes or precludes every other state of affairs. It should be obvious that exactly one possible world is actual and that at most one possible world is actual.

Corresponding to each possible world *W*, there is a set of propositions that we may call *the book on W*. A proposition is in the *book on W* just in case that state of affairs to which it corresponds is included in *W*. We might express this idea alternatively as follows: A proposition *P* is *true in a world W* if and only if *P would have been true if W had been actual*—if and only if it is not possible that *W* is actual and *P* is false. The *book on W*, then, is the set of propositions true in *W*. Books, like worlds, are maximal or complete. A book on a world is a maximal consistent set of propositions. The addition of just one proposition to it always yields an explicitly inconsistent set. There is exactly one book for each possible world.

Possible worlds possess some interesting features. For example, a proposition *p* is possible if it is true in at least one world and impossible if true in none. A proposition *p* is necessary if it is true in all possible worlds. Another feature of possible worlds is that persons as well as other things *exist* in them. Clearly, each of us exists in the actual world, but we also exist in a great many worlds distinct from the actual world. These other worlds are simply possible but unactual.[8] To say that something exists in a possible world means that it would have existed had that world been actual.

As we begin to turn our thoughts back toward God's relation to possible worlds, we must note that it would not be technically proper to say that God *creates* any possible worlds or states of affairs. What God creates are the heavens, the earth, and so forth. In performing such actions as creating the heavens and the earth and all that they contain, God brings about a multitude of states of affairs. For example, God created Socrates, but he did not create the state of affairs consisting in Socrates' existence. Strictly speaking, we must say that God *actualizes* a state of affairs, such as the state of affairs consisting in Socrates' existence. Accuracy, then, demands that we speak of God as *actualizing* a possible world, which is of course a total state of affairs.[9]

After this brief explanation of key ideas related to the logic of possible worlds, we can now return to our original question: Could God have actualized just any possible world he chose? The seventeenth-century German philosopher Gottfried Leibniz believed that it is within the scope of omnipotence to bring about any possible world.[10] Flew and Mackie, moreover, have already argued that there are possible worlds containing moral good but no moral evil. We know that

the books on such worlds form entirely consistent sets of propositions. Furthermore, as Flew and Mackie insist, if divine omnipotence
can bring about any logically possible state of affairs, even a complete
possible world, then God must be able to bring about a world containing moral good but no moral evil. Thus, God can make people so
that they always freely do what is morally right.

The Free Will Defender responds that it is not obvious that God,
though omnipotent, can bring about just any possible world he
pleases. Even granting that God is a necessary being (i.e., one that exists in every possible world), not every possible world is such that
God can actualize it.[11] In worlds in which the omnipotent God
chooses to create free persons, we must remember that the free actions of those persons cannot be determined by causal laws and antecedent conditions. More broadly, if a person is free with respect to
an action A, then God does not *bring it about* or *cause it to be the case*
that she does A or refrains from doing A. For if God *brings it about* or
causes it to be the case in any manner whatsoever that the person either
does A or does not do A, then that person is not really free.

Plantinga dubs Flew and Mackie's contention "Leibniz's Lapse." It
is the contention that

(25) God, if omnipotent, could have actualized just any possible
world he pleased.

The Free Will Defender claims to the contrary that the following is
possible:

(26) God is omnipotent, and it was not within his power to bring
about a world containing moral good but no moral evil.

Plantinga takes for granted that God cannot actualize a state of affairs
including the existence of creatures who freely take some action or
other; this would be *strong* actualization. He then considers *weak* actualization, which is all the critic really needs for his case. What is at
issue, then, is whether there is something God could have done, some
series of actions he could have taken, such that if he had, a given possible world *W* would have been actual. Let us say that *W* contains
moral good but no moral evil.

To develop his case, Plantinga provides an argument based on the
peculiar behavior of counterfactual conditionals. Rehearsing Plan-

tinga's own example, we may imagine Curley Smith, sometime mayor of Boston, who was offered a $35,000 bribe to allow a disputed freeway to be constructed. Suppose he accepted. Now, ponder:

(27)   If Curley had been offered $20,000, he would have accepted the bribe

and

(27.1)   If Curley had been offered $20,000, he would have rejected the bribe.

Next, think of the possible worlds that include the antecedent state of affairs consisting in *Curley's being offered $20,000*. Then think of two possible worlds, W and W^*, which are *exactly alike* up to the point in time when Curley responds to the bribe offer. Let us say that in W, Curley accepts the bribe, and in W^*, Curley does not. Let us call the states of affairs shared by W and W^* an initial world segment and even suppose that God could actualize this initial world segment. If Curley accepts the bribe, then God could not have actualized W^*; if Curley rejects the bribe, then God could not have actualized W. So, there is a possible world W^* in which Curley does not go wrong with respect to the bribe offer, but whether W^* is actual was partly up to Curley and not completely up to God. Therefore, we have an instance of a possible world—W^*, in this case—that God could not have brought about.

Plantinga diagnoses Curley as suffering from what he calls *transworld depravity*, a terrible malady. After defining the concept of an *individual nature* or *essence* as the set of all properties a person or thing possesses in every possible world where he or it exists, Plantinga claims that it is possible that Curley's essence suffers from transworld depravity. He states: "If an essence E suffers from transworld depravity, then it was not within God's power to actualize a possible world W such that E contains the properties *is significantly free in W* and *always does what is right in W*."[12] He then ventures the further observation: It is possible that every creaturely essence—every essence, including the property of being created by God—suffers from transworld depravity. From this, it follows that it is possible that God could not have created a world containing moral good but no moral evil.

Now the Free Will Defender has made his case against the critics. He has argued that, although there are possible worlds containing moral good but no moral evil, it is not within God's power to bring them about. Although *W** *is* possible, it is *not* possible *for God* to bring it about. This establishes that the Free Will Defender's claim that

(26) God is omnipotent, and it was not within his power to bring about a world containing moral good but no moral evil

is possible. Hence, Leibniz's Lapse—the claim that God, if omnipotent, can create any possible world—is false. The critic's case fails. Theism has been defended.

Fundamental to the Free Will Defender's case, of course, is a certain understanding of the metaphysics of freedom and its relation to divine omnipotence.[13] Theists who have an incompatibilist understanding of this matter can then defend theism by arguing that bringing about a world containing moral good but no moral evil is a cooperative venture. It requires the uncoerced concurrence of significantly free creatures; it is not up to God alone. The power of an omnipotent God is limited by the freedom he confers upon his creatures, given that he chooses to create free creatures at all.

The Current State of the Debate

It is now widely acknowledged that the Free Will Defense adequately rebuts the logical problem of evil. As it has turned out, atheistic critics made their best case that the theistic beliefs

(G) An omnipotent, omniscient, wholly good God exists

and

(E₁) Evil exists

are inconsistent. Theistic defenders—Alvin Plantinga, Keith Yandell, Stephen T. Davis, and others—articulated and amplified the Free Will Defense to show that these beliefs are not inconsistent. Thus, Version I of the logical problem has been laid to rest.

Version II in our taxonomy of the problem is based on the charge that the proposition

(G)   An omnipotent, omniscient, wholly good God exists

is inconsistent with the proposition

(E_2)   Large amounts, extreme kinds, and perplexing distributions of evil exist.

According to Plantinga, the same type of defensive maneuver used
against Version I applies to Version II. Focusing simply on the
amount of moral evil, Plantinga recommends that the theistic defender argue that something like the following claim is possible:

(28)   God is omnipotent, and it was not within his power to
bring about a world containing as much moral good and
less moral evil than this one.

Again, the theistic defender here would need to employ the same basic
assertions previously made in arguing against Version I—that God,
though omnipotent, cannot actualize a state of affairs consisting in an
agent freely doing what is right, that all creaturely essences might suffer
from transworld depravity, and so forth. A successful defense against
Version II shows, in effect, that God's existence is compatible with the
existence of as much evil as the real world does, in fact, contain.[14]
In any event, the theistic defender's strategy against all versions of
the logical problem is to show that the two key theistic beliefs in
question are not inconsistent, that they are logically compatible. This
is not to say that he must show that they are both true. This would be
too strong a requirement for the defender and inappropriate to the
nature of the issue. A kind of minimalist response is all that the purely
logical problem of evil really requires: Accusations that theism is inconsistent can be met with vindications showing that it is not.
As theists have solidified their defensive position, they have exposed
one of two fallacies by critics who advance any version of the logical
problem of evil. It appears that critics either *beg the question* by select-
ing propositions to which the theist is not committed or *lift out of
context* propositions to which the theists are committed and impute
new meanings to them that are not fully connected with the theists'
own theological background beliefs. So, the critic might find a set of
propositions that involve a logical contradiction, but doing so is irrelevant unless the propositions genuinely represent theistic belief.

In the final analysis, the logical problem of evil does not seem to be a promising avenue of attack against Christian theism. Ironically, the atheistic challenger begins by accusing the theist of committing a logical mistake and ends up embroiled in logical fallacies herself. Although Version I is by far the most popular formulation of the problem, it appears no more effective than the other two formulations. All of the formulations of the argument are now thought to exhibit certain syndromatic errors.

Admitting that the Free Will Defense is successful but remaining convinced that a viable argument from evil can still be mounted, some critics have shifted the attention to what we may call the evidential problem of evil. They agree that defense against the logical problem establishes that no claim about evil, conjoined with other key theistic beliefs, sets up an automatic contradiction. These critics maintain that, although evil does not reveal theism to be inconsistent, the facts of evil constitute evidence against theism. Using the language of possible worlds thinking, they admit that the Free Will Defense shows that there is at least one possible world in which the propositions "God exists" and "evil exists" are both true, but they maintain that this does not show that it is reasonable to think that God exists despite the evil in our world, the actual world.

Interestingly, theists seeking further understanding of the intellectual commitments of their faith have also considered whether the logical problem expresses the only rational concern related to God and evil. Thus, they also express strong interest in some kind of evidential problem of evil. The next chapters are devoted to analyzing the exact structure as well as the proper strategy for such a response.

Notes

1. Alvin Plantinga, *God and Other Minds: A Study of the Rational Justification of Belief in God* (Ithaca: Cornell University Press, 1967), pp. 131–155; Plantinga, *The Nature of Necessity* (Oxford: Clarendon Press, 1974), pp. 164–195.

2. Augustine, *On Free Choice of the Will*, trans. Anna Benjamin and L. H. Hackstaff (New York: Bobbs-Merrill, 1964), bk. 2, chap. 1, p. 36.

3. Antony Flew, "Divine Omnipotence and Human Freedom," in *New Essays in Philosophical Theology*, eds. Antony Flew and Alasdair MacIntyre (New York: Macmillan, 1955), p. 149.

4. Ibid.

5. J. L. Mackie, "Evil and Omnipotence," *Mind* 64 (1955): 209.

6. See Robert M. Adams, "Must God Create the Best?" in *The Problem of Evil: Selected Readings,* ed. Michael Peterson (Notre Dame, Ind.: University of Notre Dame Press, 1992), pp. 275–288; in the same volume, also see Philip L. Quinn, "God, Moral Perfection, and Possible Worlds," pp. 289–302.

7. The classical location of Alvin Plantinga's ideas on the logic of possible worlds and modal logic is his *Nature of Necessity,* cited in Note 1.

8. Plantinga, *God, Freedom, and Evil* (Grand Rapids, Mich.: Eerdmans, 1977), p. 39.

9. There are a multitude of things that exist but that God did not create. In addition to the fact that God has not created states of affairs, he has not created himself or numbers, propositions, properties, and so forth. These have no beginnings. God's activity results in some states of affairs being or becoming actual. See Plantinga, *The Nature of Necessity,* p. 169.

10. Gottfried Wilhelm von Leibniz, *Theodicy: Essays on the Goodness of God, the Freedom of Man, and the Origin of Evil,* ed. Austin Farrer, trans. E. M. Huggard (London: Routledge & Kegan Paul, 1952), p. 127-129.

11. From this point forward, we assume that God is a necessary and not a contingent being, that God exists in all possible worlds. The question before us, then, is whether God can actualize just any possible world that includes his existence. We follow Plantinga's discussion of which worlds God could have created, from his *Nature of Necessity,* pp. 169–174.

12. Plantinga, *God, Freedom, and Evil,* p. 53.

13. A complete statement of the Free Will Defense would need to take into account all of the elements that Plantinga builds into it, such as a concept of essences, a fuller treatment of counterfactuals of freedom, and so forth. See his *Nature of Necessity,* pp. 172ff.

14. Many thinkers, both theists and their critics, have long accepted the principle that there are no *nonlogical* limits to what an omnipotent being can do. In other words, God has the ability to bring about any *intrinsically possible* state of affairs (i.e., a state of affairs the description of which is not logically inconsistent). God could bring about, for example, white polar bears and triangles because they are intrinsically possible, but he could not bring about married bachelors and square circles because they are intrinsically impossible.

However, Plantinga revises the concept of omnipotence to allow for the fact that there are states of affairs that are possible *in themselves* (i.e., intrinsically) but that are not possible *for God* to bring about. This point depends on a proper understanding of the logic of free will. If a person is free with respect to an action, then whether she performs or refrains from performing that action is up to her, *not* God. Although a world in which all persons always freely do what is right is certainly possible, it is not a state of affairs that was within God's power to create; all of the free creatures in that world would have to help bring it about by their own choices. The Free Will Defender insists that God cannot *determine* the actions of *free* persons. See Plantinga, *The Nature of Necessity*, pp. 190–191.

For a helpful discussion of this matter, see William Wainwright, "Freedom and Omnipotence," *Nous* 2 (1968): 239–301.

Suggested Readings

Adams, Robert M. "Middle Knowledge and the Problem of Evil." *American Philosophical Quarterly* 14 (1977): 109–117.

_____. "Plantinga on the Problem of Evil." In *Alvin Plantinga*, edited by James Tomberlin and Peter van Inwagen. Dordrecht: Reidel, 1985, pp. 225–255.

Basinger, David. "Christian Theism and the Free Will Defense." *Sophia (Australia)* 19 (July 1980): 20–33.

_____. "Determinism and Evil: Some Clarifications." *Australasian Journal of Philosophy* 60 (1982): 163–164.

_____. "Divine Omniscience and the Best of All Possible Worlds." *Journal of Value Inquiry* 16 (1982): 143–148.

_____. "Human Freedom and Divine Omnipotence: Some New Thoughts on an Old Problem." *Religious Studies* 15 (1979): 491–510.

_____. "In What Sense Must God Do His Best? A Response to Hasker." *International Journal for Philosophy of Religion* 18 (1985): 161–164.

_____. "Must God Create the Best Possible World? A Response." *International Philosophical Quarterly* 20 (1980): 339–342.

Coughlan, Michael L. "The Free Will Defense and Natural Evil." *International Journal for Philosophy of Religion* 20 (1986): 93–108.

Gale, Richard. "Freedom and the Free Will Defense." *Social Theory and Practice* (Fall 1990): 397–423.

_____. *On the Nature and Existence of God*. Cambridge: Cambridge University Press, 1991.

Hasker, William. "Must God Do His Best?" *International Journal for Philosophy of Religion* 16 (1984): 213–224.

Hoitenga, Dewey. "Logic and the Problem of Evil." *American Philosophical Quarterly* 4 (1967): 114–126.

Kane, G. Stanley. "The Free-Will Defense Defended." *The New Scholasticism* 50 (1976): 435–446.

Mavrodes, George. "The Problem of Evil." In *Belief in God: A Study in the Epistemology of Religion*. New York: Random House, 1970, chap. 4.

Oakes, Robert A. "Actualities, Possibilities, and Free-Will Theodicy." *The New Scholasticism* 46 (1972): 191–201.

Pike, Nelson. "Plantinga on Free Will and Evil." *Religious Studies* 15 (1979): 449–473.

Plantinga, Alvin. "Existence, Necessity, and God." *The New Scholasticism* 50 (1976): 61–72.

_____. "The Free Will Defense." In *Philosophy in America,* edited by Max Black. London: George Allen and Unwin, 1965.

_____. *God and Other Minds: A Study of the Rational Justification of Belief in God.* Ithaca: Cornell University Press, 1967.

_____. *God, Freedom, and Evil.* Grand Rapids, Mich.: Eerdmans, 1977.

_____. *The Nature of Necessity.* Oxford: Clarendon Press, 1974.

_____. "Which Worlds Could God Have Created?" *Journal of Philosophy* 70 (1973): 539–552.

Quinn, Philip L. "God, Moral Perfection, and Possible Worlds." In *God: The Contemporary Discussion,* edited by Frederick Sontag and M. Darrol Bryant. New York: Rose of Sharon Press, 1982, pp. 197–213.

Rowe, William L. "Plantinga on Possible Worlds and Evil." *Journal of Philosophy* 70 (1973): 554–555.

Sennett, James F. "The Free Will Defense and Determinism." *Faith and Philosophy* 8 (1991): 340–353.

Smart, Ninian. "Omnipotence, Evil and Supermen." *Philosophy* 36 (1961): 188–195.

Stewart, Melville. *The Greater-Good Defense: An Essay on the Rationality of Faith.* New York: St. Martin's, 1993.

Wainwright, William. "Christian Theism and the Free Will Defense." *International Journal for Philosophy of Religion* 6 (1975): 243–250.

Walls, Jerry. "The Free Will Defense, Calvinism, Wesley, and the Goodness of God." *Christian Scholar's Review* 13 (January 1983): 19–33.

4

The Probabilistic
Problem of Evil

From the atheistic critics' point of view, the beauty of the logical argument from evil is that, if it could be made to work, it would be a tour de force for atheism. Critics could then ignore any allegedly favorable evidence for God's existence and declare theism patently irrational. However, with what appears to be the decisive defeat of the logical argument from evil by the Free Will Defense,[1] some critics have developed a different kind of argument from evil. This other type of argument seeks to establish that the existence of God is still somehow rationally unacceptable given the facts of evil. Philosophers wielding this kind of argument say that evil somehow counts against the existence of God, although it is not inconsistent with the existence of God. Since the mid-1970s, the number of these arguments in the philosophical literature has grown significantly. Such arguments have been variously labeled evidential, inductive, or a posteriori,[2] but one of the more prominent formulations is now called the probabilistic argument from evil. It is to this argument that I now turn, leaving consideration of a more broadly conceived evidential argument until the next chapter.

An Initial Skirmish

Proponents of the probabilistic argument maintain that evil makes the existence of God *improbable* or *unlikely*. Let us consider an early exchange between nontheistic and theistic philosophers along these lines. Consider how J. W. Cornman and Keith Lehrer present the problem in the guise of a provocative thought experiment:

If you were all-good, all-knowing, and all-powerful and you were going to create a universe in which there were sentient beings—beings that are happy and sad; enjoy pleasure, feel pain; express love, anger, pity, hatred—what kind of world would you create? . . . Try to imagine what such a world would be like. Would it be like the one which actually does exist, this world we live in? Would you create a world such as this one if you had the power and know-how to create any logically possible world? If your answer is "no," as it seems to be, then you should begin to understand why the evil of suffering and pain in this world is such a problem for anyone who thinks God created this world. . . . Given this world, then, it seems, we should conclude that it is *improbable* that it was created or sustained by anything we would call God. Thus, given this particular world, it seems that we should conclude that it is *improbable* that God—who, if he exists, created the world—exists. Consequently, the belief that God does not exist, rather than the belief that he exists, would seem to be *justified by the evidence* we find in this world.[3]

Here we find the language of probability. Cornman and Lehrer are saying that evil in the world makes the existence of God *improbable*. But let us try to extract the essential argument from their comments. Before proceeding, we shall discount at the outset the rhetorical suggestion that the reader's answer "seems" to be a negative one. This phraseology imposes a bias on the reader and too hastily dismisses a number of very important perspectives about why the world contains evil. I shall cover some of these perspectives later but here must clarify the structure of the argument at hand.

One premise in Cornman and Lehrer's argument seems to be

(29) If God is omnipotent and omniscient, then he could have created any logically possible world.

Another premise seems to be

(30) If God is all-good, he would choose to create the best world he could.

From (29) and (30), they conclude

(31) If God is omniscient, omnipotent, and all-good, he would have created the best of all possible worlds.

Then they add

(32) It is unlikely or improbable that the actual world is the best of all possible worlds.

And from (31) and (32), it follows that

(33) It is unlikely or improbable that there is an omnipotent, omniscient, and all-good God.

If this is a reasonably accurate sketch of the basic moves of the argument,[4] how might theists respond?

Alvin Plantinga thinks that the argument contains at least two major errors. For one, Cornman and Lehrer incorporate into their argument Leibniz's Lapse—the claim that God, if omnipotent, can create any logically possible world. We have already seen the error of Leibniz's Lapse in our discussion of the Free Will Defense for the logical problem. Thus, Plantinga maintains that the argument as stated is not sound because it incorporates this falsehood. We now know that it is simply not true that God, if he exists, could have actualized any possible world. Another error in the argument is that it seems to presuppose that there *is* "a best of all possible worlds," a concept that is incoherent. Consider what we all know: that for any prime number you designate, there is always one that is greater. In like manner, Plantinga reasons that, for any world you mention (with however many dancing girls and deliriously happy sentient creatures), there is always one that is better (with even more dancing girls and deliriously happy sentient creatures). So, Plantinga pronounces the argument of Cornman and Lehrer incapable of showing that the existence of evil in the world makes it unlikely that God exists.

A Modified Probability Argument

We might, however, try to modify and strengthen Cornman and Lehrer's argument in order to make the best of their case against theism. One way to revise it is to eliminate the claim that God can create just any logically possible world. The substitute claim can be made that, among the logically possible worlds that were within God's

power to create, he could have created one containing a more favorable balance of good and evil. Another alteration would be to cast
this claim in terms of *natural* evil rather than moral evil, since many
thinkers now grant that God could not do anything about the
amount of moral evil brought about by free human beings. Nevertheless, they still insist that God can control the amount of natural evil.
With these two adjustments, does the argument fare any better?

Plantinga thinks that the modified argument still fails. He rebuts
this stronger rendition of the argument by extending the Free Will
Defense—the claim that it is possible that God cannot actualize any
possible world that includes free agency. His point is that the evil in
the world does *not* render the existence of God improbable. He asks
us to consider the following proposition:

(34) All the evil in this world is broadly moral evil; and of all the
worlds God could have created, none contains a better balance of broadly moral good with respect to broadly moral
evil.

In keeping with the earlier strategy of defense, Plantinga asks us to
consider that (34) is logically possible.

The reference to "broadly moral evil" requires comment. Plantinga
claims it is possible that what we normally call natural evil is really
broadly moral evil caused by nonhuman free agents.[5] Traditional religion, for example, attributes much evil to Satan or to Satan and his
cohorts. These demonic spirits are fallen angels who seek to spoil
God's creation. In this light, Plantinga states that, of all the worlds
God could have created, it is possible that none contains a better balance of broadly moral good and broadly moral evil than this one.

Although we may have no evidence to confirm (34), Plantinga
points out that we do not appear to have any evidence that would disconfirm it either. But how shall we think about this whole business of
confirmation anyway? Let us say that a proposition *p confirms* a
proposition *q* if *q* is more probable than not on *p* alone: if, that is, *q*
would be more probable that not-*q* with respect to what we know, if
p were the only thing we knew that was relevant to *q*. And let us say
that *p disconfirms q* if *p* confirms the denial of *q*.

Although there is really no way to measure the quantity of evil in the
world, Plantinga takes Cornman and Lehrer's argument to be about
the *amount* and *variety* of evil. He then advances this proposition:

(35) There are 10^{13} turps of evil.

Plantinga here coins the term "turp" as a basic unit of evil in order to facilitate discussion. Here the expression "10^{13} turps" names the past, present, and future evil in the actual world.

Claiming that (35) does not disconfirm (34), Plantinga goes on to say that neither does it disconfirm the following:

(36) God is omniscient, omnipotent, and morally perfect; God has created the world; all the evil in the world is broadly moral evil; and there is no possible world God could have created that contains a better balance of broadly moral good and broadly moral evil.

Now, if a proposition p confirms a proposition q, then it confirms every proposition q entails; and if p disconfirms q, p disconfirms every proposition that entails q. It seems clear that (35) does not disconfirm (36); but (36) entails

(37) God is omniscient, omnipotent, and morally perfect.

So, the existence of the great amount and variety of evil does not render improbable the existence of an omniscient, omnipotent, and wholly good God. Of course, there may be *other* things we know such that the existence of God is improbable with respect to *them*. Nonetheless, the amount and variety of evil in this world does not disconfirm God's existence.

Here we can see how the Free Will Defense works against the probabilistic problem of evil. Against the logical problem, of course, Plantinga established that

(G) An omnipotent, omniscient, wholly good God exists

and

(E_1) Evil exists

are not logically incompatible. He accomplished this by showing that the consistent conjunction of a certain proposition about free will and a proposition asserting God's existence entails that there is evil. Now, against the probabilistic problem, Plantinga employs a similar defensive strategy to show that

(G) An omnipotent, omniscient, wholly good God exists

and

(35) There are 10^{13} turps of evil

are not probabilistically incompatible.[6] He does this by showing that proposition (G) and a certain proposition about all evil being broadly moral evil entail that God could not control the evil in the world.

Some critics as well as some theists have misunderstood Plantinga's suggestion that possibly there are nonhuman free agents—what traditional religion calls "demons" or "fallen angels"—who are responsible for what we call natural evil. This would, in effect, make all evil broadly moral evil. Several thinkers rightly pointed out that neither classical theism nor the living religions that embrace it (Christianity, Judaism, or Islam) hold that demonic activity is the best explanation of evil. Yet there is a misunderstanding here that provides an opportunity to clarify the nature of Plantinga's defensive strategy against the charge that God could reduce the amount of evil. Plantinga does not *postulate* that there are nonhuman free creatures who create evil in our world; he is not offering this notion as a hypothesis in order to *explain* anything. Plantinga's defensive strategy does not require that the claim that all natural evil could be viewed as broadly moral evil be *true* or even *probably true*. And he certainly does not have to be committed to its truth or even its probable truth. In light of a sophisticated theistic worldview, it could even be factually *false* that demons create what we call natural evil; or, in light of many other things we know, it could be *highly improbable*. But Plantinga's strategy requires only that it be *possible* and consistent with (G) in order to accomplish its defensive purpose.[7]

Three Probabilistic Arguments from Evil

Discussion of the prospects for a viable probabilistic argument from evil did not end with Plantinga's critique of Cornman and Lehrer. Several atheistic critics have developed their own statements of the argument. The general strategy they follow is to argue that a proposition such as

(E) A great amount and variety of evil exists

is evidence against the proposition

(G) An omnipotent, omniscient, wholly good God exists.

Philosophers have still thought it worthwhile to continue to probe the issue of exactly how it is that (E) renders (G) improbable. In fact, the probabilistic argument from evil could be framed and subsequently analyzed in terms of any of the three (E)-propositions discussed in Chapter 2. But we will pursue the argument that incorporates (E) as stated here.

After all, what is the relationship that the critic says holds between (E) and (G) when he says the former is evidence against the latter or that (~G), which is the denial of (G), is probable with respect to (E)? In probability studies generally, the probability of any proposition B on the basis of the evidence A is depicted as $P(B/A)$. The question, then, is how to understand precisely how all of this works in the matter of God and evil—that is, how to interpret the critic's claim that $P((G)/(E))$ is low, less than .5. To comprehend this, of course, we must have some idea of what the relationship is between any propositions B and A when A *is evidence for* B or when B *is probable with respect to* A. Yet this whole area of scholarship is notoriously unsettled, with no clear consensus on how to define the evidential relationship between propositions or on how to think about the probability of one proposition given another proposition. Plantinga suggests that a good starting place would be to view the relationship between propositions B and A as conforming to the calculus of probabilities. He then considers the three main interpretations of probability—personalist, logical, and frequency—to determine if there is any basis for a good probabilistic argument from evil.[8] Let us briefly review his remarks about the first two interpretations and then focus on how he treats the third.

According to a *personalist interpretation*, the probability of (G) on (E) reflects a person's *credence function*, which is the degree of belief that she assigns to a given proposition, $P(A)$, or that she assigns to the proposition *given* another proposition, $P(A/B)$. Plantinga pronounces a personalist argument for the low probability of theism based on evil to be nothing more than mere biographical information. Predictably, an atheist will assign a low subjective probability, perhaps close to zero, to the hypothesis that God exists—either on its own terms or in view of the evidence as he sees it. So, it is not surprising that the atheistic critic maintains that $Ps((G)/(E)) = < .5$. A theist, on the other hand, will assign a high subjective probability to (G)—either on its own terms or in view of the evidence as she sees it. But then it appears that a personalistic probability argument from evil tells only about the belief dispositions of the atheistic critic and nothing about whether God exists or whether it is rational per se to believe that God exists given the evidence of evil.[9]

Plantinga maintains that an evidential argument based on the *logical theory* of probability fares no better than the personalistic argument. Here probability is a "quasi-logical relation of which entailment is a special case."[10] Trying to protect probability judgments from the taint of subjectivity, those promoting this theory think of probability as a kind of "partial entailment" of one proposition by another.[11] In other words, one proposition (A) has an a priori probability in view of another proposition (B). The ideally rational person, then, should believe (A) to the exact degree it is entailed by (B). For example, the probability of the proposition

(38) Friedrich cannot swim

given

(39) Nine out of ten Prussians cannot swim and Friedrich is a
     Prussian/German

appears to be .9—i.e., $P((38)/(39)) = .9$. So, the rational person who knows nothing else relevant will believe (38) to the degree .9. However, if we consider

(40) Friedrich is a lifeguard,

then the probability of (38) changes dramatically!

Likewise, the critic offering an argument from evil rooted in the logical theory of probability might claim that the probability of

(G) An omnipotent, omniscient, wholly good God exists

is low given, say,

(E$_1$) Evil exists.

But the theist might retort that the probability of (G) changes significantly when we consider

(R) God has a morally sufficient reason for allowing evil to exist.

It is extremely difficult to see, therefore, how a given proposition can just *have* a certain probability on the basis of another proposition—a matter long debated among scholars of inductive logic.[12] Since there is no reason to think that contingent propositions have a priori probabilities, Plantinga concludes that there is no reason to think that a proposition such as (E$_1$) disconfirms (G).

Although the personalist and logical theories of probability do not seem to lend themselves to making a decent atheistic argument from evil, a number of thinkers have considered whether *frequency theory* (or statistical probability) offers a more interesting and more promising way of framing the argument. According to the frequency theory, probability is a *ratio*: It is a measure of the relative frequency with which the members of a specified class of objects or events exhibit a certain property.[13] An insurance actuary, for example, might compute the number of thirty-year-old males in a sample of 10,000 who survive to their fortieth birthdays and get a result of 9,450. The probability value, then, is .945. This value, in turn, becomes a predictive factor for the underwriter in setting insurance rates. There are literally thousands of situations in science, mathematics, and practical life in which this kind of statistical reasoning is entirely appropriate and helpful.

Wesley Salmon suggests that the frequency theory can also be used to conclude that evil makes God's existence improbable—that is, P((G)/(E)) = < .5.[14] But how are we to understand this probabilistic claim in frequency terms? Salmon must surely mean something like the following: Among possible worlds that contain as much evil as this one does (which is 10^{13} turps), there are relatively few—less than half—that are divinely created.[15] Thus, proposition

(G) An omnipotent, omniscient, wholly good God exists

has a low probability value, i.e., below .5. But how would one arrive at such a judgment? Should we start by imagining hypothetical universes (or what we have called "possible worlds") and simply estimating how many containing as much evil as this one were created by a being who has the relevant theistic attributes? Salmon would insist that the number here would be relatively low.

Plantinga points out a number of serious difficulties in the frequentist methods Salmon uses for arriving at the conclusion that $P((G)/(E)) = < .5$. For one thing, how can the frequentist critic count the possible worlds, which are theoretically infinite in number, so that he may perform his calculations? For another thing, what about the differences in how the theist and atheist make a number of initial assessments before arriving at a final value for $P((G)/(E))$? After all, the nontheist would typically assess the probability that there would be less evil in our world if God did exist to be high, whereas the theist would most certainly disagree.

Here Plantinga recognizes the fact that such initial assessments are ultimately relative to the *total belief set* that each party brings to the probability judgment at hand and that the belief sets of the theist and the critic differ in some irreconcilable ways.[16] We would expect the theist and the atheistic critic to disagree, for instance, on the success of various independent arguments for God's existence, such as the ontological and cosmological arguments.[17] But surely, their assessments of such matters will form part of their respective total belief sets, or, as Plantinga calls them, their respective "noetic frameworks." These as well as other problems undercut any effort to mount a viable frequency argument from evil.[18]

Reformed Epistemology and Evil

In the contemporary debates over God and evil, a certain pattern of response has emerged in regard to both the logical and the probabilistic arguments: challenge from the critic followed by defensive maneuvers by the theist. In discussions of the logical argument, the critic charges that belief in God and belief in evil are *inconsistent*. The theist shields his belief system from the charge by demonstrating that theism is *not inconsistent*. In discussions of the probabilistic argument, the critic claims that God's existence is *improbable* in light of the evil in the world. The theist answers by showing that God's existence is *not improbable* given evil. These defensive responses are technically correct and instructive in many ways. We should note that such responses are not geared to show that theism is plausible, probable, or true. They are also not aimed at showing either that theism makes good sense on its own terms or that it makes better sense than competing worldviews. The general defensive strategy is simply that of protecting theistic beliefs while deflecting all challenges—a strategy that has become well recognized and widely employed.

Interestingly, theists who have constructed defenses against various challenges detected a recurring flaw in critics' attacks. In defending against the logical problem of evil, theists took exception to auxiliary assumptions employed by their atheistic critics who sought to deduce a contradiction within theism. As we have seen, these critics constructed their arguments using propositions defining such theistic concepts as omnipotence and perfect goodness—definitions that tilted the controversy in their favor from the outset. This, of course, was an early indication of how different thinkers inevitably appeal to their own background information in evaluating philosophical positions. Then, in defending against the probabilistic problem of evil, theistic defenders pointed out that the atheistic critic could not avoid assessing a number of probabilities based on things he already accepts, whereas the theist would clearly differ on such things. So, predictably, (G) will be improbable with respect to things that the atheist accepts but probable with respect to things that the theist accepts.

Continuing reflection on the construction of both logical and probabilistic arguments has brought to light an important fact—that

(G) An omnipotent, omniscient, wholly good God exists

must be probabilistically assessed on the basis of all the propositions one knows or believes. This is what we mean when we talk of the requirement of "total evidence." Discussions of this matter have become couched in terms of one's "epistemic framework" or "noetic structure." But then, it is difficult to see how so many of the arguments from evil—both logical and probabilistic—are really objections against *theism* when they are based on the atheistic critic's total set of beliefs. How might we think of the objection from evil now?

Clearly, the discussion shifts away from its original focus on whether (E₁) or (E) or any other (E)-like proposition per se probabilistically disconfirms the proposition that God exists. Instead, the controversy revolves around a whole context of other beliefs within which such a probabilistic judgment could ever be made. We may call this context of total evidence one's *evidence set*. So, if there is going to be any kind of effective probabilistic argument from evil, it will have to run along these lines: For any theist T, there is a set of propositions Ts that constitute his *total evidence set*; for any proposition A that the theist accepts, he is rational in accepting A only if A is not improbable with respect to Ts. The critic's case, then, is that the existence of God *is* improbable with respect to Ts.

Many philosophers—including David Hume, W. K. Clifford, Bertrand Russell, Antony Flew, Michael Scriven, and others—make this kind of case.[19] Flew maintains that it is rational to presume that atheism is true (i.e., that theism is false) unless convincing arguments for theism are advanced.[20] This places the burden of proof on the theist, since there are propositions that all rational persons believe or ought to believe that either offer no support for (G) or make it improbable. According to most critics, then, the theist is irrational (and perhaps unethical) in believing in God because there is little or no evidence for the belief (e.g., the failure of traditional theistic proofs) and because there is impressive evidence (e.g., evil) against the belief. At this juncture, a number of important questions surface, questions about what beliefs are properly included in a well-formed noetic structure, what it means to be rationally entitled to hold a belief, and what our epistemic obligations are.

In addressing such questions, Alvin Plantinga, Nicholas Wolterstorff, William Alston, and George Mavrodes have developed a position known as Reformed epistemology.[21] Reformed epistemology is relevant, first, to the critic's procedure of formulating reasons for not believing (G) and, second, to the critic's protest that defense against these reasons is an unsatisfying minimalist approach. Plantinga and other Reformed epistemologists explain that the critic operates on the *evidentialist* assumption that a person is rationally warranted in holding a belief only if he holds other beliefs that give it good evidential support. Conversely, one is not rationally warranted in holding a belief if there is good evidence against it. Of course, "evidence" here must be expanded to include one's total evidence set. This is a very natural way of thinking about *rationality*.

Of course, the critic here takes the probabilistic argument from evil to supply good evidence against (G). When the theist provides a defense showing that evil does not count *against* it, the critic points out that the theist is not entitled to hold (G) unless he can supply good evidence *for* it. It is this whole evidentialist way of looking at the matter that Reformed epistemology calls into question. Reformed epistemologists point out that those evidentialists who raise serious challenges to theism also accept *strong foundationalism*. Strong foundationalism is a way of looking at human knowledge as built or erected upon "foundations." The general foundationalist position, then, is that our beliefs may be divided into two kinds: those that are supported by or receive evidential support from other beliefs and those that are accepted without being supported by still other beliefs. This second kind of belief forms the "basis" on which our entire structure of belief and knowledge ultimately rests. Foundational beliefs are "basic" and not "derived" from other beliefs.[22]

The "strong" foundationalist wants to place very strict requirements on what sorts of beliefs can be in the foundations. Wanting to allow only beliefs about which it is impossible or nearly impossible to go wrong, the foundationalist asserts that the only beliefs that can be properly basic are those that are either *self-evident* or *incorrigible*. Self-evident beliefs are seen to be true by anyone who understands them (e.g., the simple truths of arithmetic, such as $2 + 2 = 4$). Incorrigible beliefs are those that deal with one's immediate experience and thus are thought to be immune from serious doubt (e.g., reports of consciousness, such as "I am feeling pain" and "I seem to be seeing something green"). A strong foundationalist, then, maintains that

(SF) A person is rational in accepting a given belief only if that belief is self-evident or incorrigible or is derived form self-evident or incorrigible beliefs using acceptable methods of logical inference.

The "evidentialist challenge" to religious belief, then, is for religious belief to satisfy these requirements of evidence.

Many nontheists (e.g., W. K. Clifford, Antony Flew, and others) embrace evidentialism and strong foundationalism, but a number of well-known theists do as well (e.g., Descartes, Locke, and Leibniz). Historically, the twin assumptions of evidentialism and strong foundationalism have created a certain way of thinking about how religious belief must be justified. The theistic evidentialist is obliged to give positive evidence for belief in the existence of God, whereas the evidentialist critic either must provide evidence for rejecting belief in God or must point out that the theist's evidence is insufficient.

Plantinga has identified two serious difficulties with strong foundationalism. For one thing, strong foundationalism is self-referentially incoherent. It simply does not meet its own standards of evidence, for it is not self-evident, incorrigible, or logically derivable from beliefs that are. For another thing, strong foundationalism is overly restrictive in regard to what kinds of beliefs can count as properly basic. Strong foundationalism mistakenly rules out various kinds of beliefs that are properly basic but that are neither self-evident nor incorrigible. In fact, a careful analysis of our native noetic powers (such as perception and memory) shows that they produce *immediate* or *direct* beliefs in us. Such beliefs as "I see a tree in the quad now" and "I had breakfast three hours ago" are "properly basic" for me although they are not held on the basis of other beliefs in my evidential set. When one is in normal circumstances and one's cognitive powers are functioning properly, one is entitled to accept the beliefs formed by these native cognitive powers, such as perception and memory.

Now we are ready to understand the Reformed epistemologists' contention that belief in God can be a properly basic belief. Plantinga suggests that all rational persons have cognitive faculties that, under appropriate conditions, can form such a belief in them. Thus, I might accept the belief that

(41) There is such a person as God

without appeal to my other beliefs. That is, it can be part of the foundations of my noetic structure without being derived by arguments from foundational beliefs.

The relevance of Reformed epistemology to the discussion of God and evil is that it changes how we think about the rationality of the parties involved. And it is a natural component in defensive maneuvers by theists. For one thing, Reformed epistemology explains how the theist may be rational without mounting, say, a probabilistic argument *for* divine existence that is aimed at overturning the probabilistic argument from evil. The theist may simply hold belief in God as basic (without argument). Then, when a critic advances some version of the problem of evil and the theist feels its probative force, the theist must deal with the objection. The objection is a potential *defeater* of the basic belief in God; it threatens the theist's noetic structure. But the only action rationally required of the theist, according to Reformed epistemology, is to *defeat* the defeater, so to speak. This may be done by *defense*, showing that the critic's case against theism does not succeed, whatever that case may be (e.g., logical or probabilistic problem of evil). Of course, it is entirely possible for the antitheistic critic to respond by trying to defeat the defeater defeater and so on. Thus, although one may be rational in believing in God without discursive reasoning and argument, this would be a situation in which reasoning and argument is needed. However, the point of theistic argumentation in this case has changed from the positive enterprise of showing that belief in God is rational because it is derived from basic beliefs to the project of showing that antitheistic attacks do not reveal it to be rationally substandard.

Notes

1. Among nontheistic philosophers who recognize that the logical problem is not effective are: Edward Madden and Peter Hare, *Evil and the Concept of God* (Springfield, Ill.: Charles C. Thomas, 1968), and William Rowe, *Philosophy of Religion* (Encino and Belmont, Calif.: Dickenson, 1978).

2. For the inductive argument, see Bruce Reichenbach, "The Inductive Argument from Evil," *American Philosophical Quarterly* 17 (1980): 221–227; for the a posteriori argument, see Alvin Plantinga, *God and Other Minds: A Study of the Rational Justification of Belief in God* (Ithaca: Cornell University, 1967), p. 128.

3. James W. Cornman and Keith Lehrer, *Philosophical Problems and Arguments: An Introduction* (New York: Macmillan, 1970), pp. 340–341 (italics mine).

4. Here we follow Plantinga's way of outlining the argument. See Plantinga, *God, Freedom, and Evil* (Grand Rapids, Mich.: Eerdmans, 1977), pp. 59–64.

5. Plantinga first introduced the notion of all evil being broadly moral evil in dealing with the argument that the existence of God is inconsistent with the existence of natural evil. This notion is then available to be imported into his discussion of the probabilistic problem.

6. Plantinga, *God, Freedom, and Evil*, p. 64.

7. Of course, classical theism as well as the major monotheistic religions that espouse it acknowledge that God's fruitful and creative power can create many orders of rational, free beings other than human beings. What is repugnant both to common sense and to a sophisticated theological understanding is the notion that reference to nonhuman creatures who are rational and free plays a major part in the explanation of the evil we experience. One can add to this the assessment that it is extremely unlikely that what we call natural evil in our world is really broadly moral evil. First, natural law themes can be drawn from biblical sources as well as major theologies of the Christian faith. Such themes envisage the natural world as constituted by impersonal objects operating and

interacting according to their own inherent natures. Second, denial of or at least de-emphasis on the role of demons or devils in our world can be adduced from such sources by fair and intelligent interpretation.

8. Alvin Plantinga, "The Probabilistic Argument from Evil," *Philosophical Studies* 35 (1979): 1–53. For those wishing to follow the subsequent discussions of Plantinga's work in this area, see Keith Chrzan, "Plantinga on Atheistic Induction," *Sophia* 27 (1988): 10, and Plantinga, "Epistemic Probability and Evil," *Archivio di filosofia* 56 (1988), reprinted in Daniel Howard-Snyder, ed., *The Evidential Argument from Evil* (Bloomington: Indiana University Press, 1996), pp. 69–96.

9. Plantinga, "Probabilistic Argument," pp. 15–18.

10. Ibid., p. 15.

11. Ibid., p. 18.

12. Plantinga thoroughly discusses this and other difficulties in ibid., pp. 21–30.

13. Of course, the classical or LaPlacean theory of probability also assumes it is a ratio but one established a priori based on equiprobable outcomes.

14. Wesley Salmon, "Religion and Science: A New Look at Hume's *Dialogues*," *Philosophical Studies* 33 (1978): 143–176. Actually, Salmon proposes that we evaluate the design argument claim that it is highly probable that this world was created by a benevolent, intelligent Supreme Being. In evaluating the argument from the perspective of frequency theory, he concludes that it is improbable that this world was designed by an all-knowing, all-powerful, and all-good being, particularly given the evil that it contains.

15. Plantinga, "Probabilistic Argument," p. 33. In the same article (pp. 32–39), Plantinga also considers the possibility that the frequency claim here involves the frequency with which one class of propositions are true relative to another class of propositions.

16. Plantinga also calls these belief sets "noetic structures" and makes important observations on how they function in human knowledge. See his "Probabilistic Argument," pp. 44, 48, and 51.

17. See Michael Peterson, William Hasker, Bruce Reichenbach, and David Basinger, *Reason and Religious Belief: An Introduction to the Philosophy of Religion,* 2nd ed. (New York: Oxford University Press, 1998), pp. 87–91 and 91–100.

18. For more criticism of the frequentist argument advanced by Salmon, see Nancy Cartwright, "Comments on Wesley Salmon's 'Science and Religion: A New Look at Hume's *Dialogues*,'" *Philosophical Studies* 33 (1978): 177–183.

Although frequentist methods may not be feasible for arriving at crucial initial assessments or estimates that can, in turn, be used in calculating the probability of (G), Bruce Reichenbach, a theist, still thinks it worthwhile to consider Salmon's proposal that Bayes's Theorem be used for calculation purposes. Where P(B/A) means the probability of B on A, Reichenbach formulates Bayes's Theorem in this fashion:

$$P(B/A\&C) = \frac{P(B/A) \times P(C/A\&B)}{[P(B/A) \times P(C/A\&B)] + [P(\bar{B}/A) \times P(C/A\&\bar{B})]}.$$

The parts of the theorem have the following meanings:

P(B/A) =   the *prior probability* that the original hypothesis is true, given the background evidence

P($\bar{B}$/A) =   the *prior probability* that the original hypothesis is false, given the background evidence

P(C/A&B) =   the probability that the effect will be observed, given that the hypothesis is true

P(C/A&$\bar{B}$) =   the probability that the effect will be observed, given that the hypothesis is false

P(B/A&C) =   the probability that the hypothesis is true, given the background evidence and the fact that the effect is observed.

Now the way is prepared for construing a probabilistic argument from evil along Bayesian lines.

Reichenbach sets up the framework for the Bayesian-type argument from evil:

$$P((G)/(N)\&(E)) = \frac{P((G)/(N)) \times P((E)/(N)\&(G))}{[P((G)/(N)) \times P((E)/(N)\&(G))] + [P((\bar{G})/(N)) \times P((E)/(N)\&(\bar{G}))]}.$$

Then, casting the critic's argument in terms of the amount of natural evil in our world, Reichenbach interprets the parts of the theorem as follows:

P((G)/(N)) =   the probability that a personal, loving, omnipotent, omniscient, perfectly good God exists, given the furniture and structure of the world (including sentient creatures, insentient creatures, physical objects, and laws of nature but *excluding* any morally sufficient reason, defense or theodicy for evil, any construed evidence for God's existence, or evil)

P(($\bar{G}$)/(N)) =   the probability that a God as described above does not exist, given the furniture and structure of the world

P((E)/(N)&(G)) =   the probability of there being the amount of evil that exists in our world, given that the world described above obtains and the God described above exists

$P((E)/(N)\&(\bar{G})) =$ the probability of there being the amount of evil that exists in our world, given that the world described above obtains and the God described above does not exist

$P((G)/(N)\&(E)) =$ the probability that God as described above exists, given that the world described above obtains and there exists the amount of natural evil that our world contains.

Of course, the critic advancing this kind of Bayesian argument claims, in the end, that $P((G)/(N)\&(E)) = < .5$.

Reichenbach rightly observes that $P((G)/(N)\&(E))$ cannot be computed by the atheistic critic without determining the *prior probabilities*, $P((G)/(N))$ and $P((\bar{G})/(N))$.

For fuller context, see Bruce Reichenbach, *Evil and a Good God* (New York: Fordham University Press, 1982), pp. 26–27.

19. W. K. Clifford, "The Ethics of Belief," in his *Lectures and Essays* (London: Macmillan, 1979), pp. 345f; Brand Blanchard, *Reason and Belief* (London: Allen & Unwin, 1974), pp. 400f; Bertrand Russell, "Why I Am Not a Christian," in his *Why I Am Not a Christian* (New York: Simon & Schuster, 1957), pp. 3ff; Michael Scriven, *Primary Philosophy* (New York: McGraw-Hill, 1966), pp. 87ff; Antony Flew, *The Presumption of Atheism* (London: Pemberton, 1976), pp. 22ff.

W. K. Clifford insists that "it is wrong always, everywhere, and for anyone to believe anything upon insufficient evidence." See his "Ethics," p. 186.

20. Flew, *Presumption,* pp. 14–15.

21. See, for example, their respective essays in Alvin Plantinga and Nicholas Wolterstorff, eds., *Faith and Rationality: Reason and Belief in God* (Notre Dame, Ind.: University of Notre Dame Press, 1983). See also Alvin Plantinga, "The Reformed Objection to Natural Theology," *Christian Scholars Review* 11 (1982): 187–198.

22. See the fuller discussion of evidentialism and foundationalism in Peterson et al., *Reason,* pp. 146–165.

Suggested Readings

Adams, Robert M. "Plantinga on the Problem of Evil." In *Alvin Plantinga,* edited by James Tomberlin and Peter van Inwagen. Dordrecht: Reidel, 1985, pp. 225–255.

Basinger, David. "Evil as Evidence Against the Existence of God: A Response." *Philosophy Research Archives* 4 (1978): article no. 1275.

Cartwright, Nancy. "Comments on Wesley Salmon's 'Science and Religion.'" *Philosophical Studies* 33 (Fall 1978): 177–183.

Chrzan, Keith. "Plantinga on Atheistic Induction." *Sophia (Australia)* 27 (July 1988): 10–14.

Draper, Paul. "Evil and the Proper Basicality of Belief in God." *Faith and Philosophy* 8 (1991): 135–147.

_____. "Pain and Pleasure: An Evidential Problem for Theists." *Nous* 23 (1989): 331–350.

_____. "Probabilistic Arguments from Evil." *Religious Studies* 28 (1993): 303–317.

Howard-Snyder, Daniel. *The Evidential Argument from Evil.* Bloomington: Indiana University Press, 1996.

Kaufman, Gordon D. "Evidentialism: A Theologian's Response." *Faith and Philosophy* 6 (1989): 35–46.

Martin, Michael. *Atheism: A Philosophical Justification.* Philadelphia: Temple University Press, 1990.

_____. "God, Satan and Natural Evil." *Sophia (Australia)* 22 (October 1983): 43–45.

_____. "Is Evil Evidence Against the Existence of God?" *Mind* 87 (1978): 429–432.

_____. "A Theistic Inductive Argument from Evil?" *International Journal for Philosophy of Religion* 22 (1987): 81–87.

Oakes, Robert A. "God, Suffering, and Conclusive Evidence." *Sophia (Australia)* 14 (July 1975): 16–20.

Peterson, Michael. "Recent Work on the Problem of Evil." *American Philosophical Quarterly* 20 (1983): 321–339.

Peterson, Michael L., ed. *The Problem of Evil: Selected Readings.* Notre Dame, Ind.: University of Notre Dame Press, 1992.

Peterson, Michael, William Hasker, Bruce Reichenbach, and David Basinger. *Reason and Religious Belief: An Introduction to the Philosophy of Religion.* 2nd ed. New York: Oxford University Press, 1998, chap. 6.

Plantinga, Alvin. "Epistemic Probability and Evil." *Archivio di filosofia* (Italy) 56 (1988): 557–584.

_____. *God, Freedom, and Evil.* Grand Rapids, Mich.: Eerdmans, 1977.

_____. *The Nature of Necessity.* Oxford: Clarendon Press, 1974.

_____. "The Probabilistic Argument from Evil." *Philosophical Studies* 35 (1979): 1–53.

Reichenbach, Bruce. *Evil and a Good God.* New York: Fordham University Press, 1982.

_____. "The Inductive Argument from Evil." *American Philosophical Quarterly* 17 (1980): 221–227.

Salmon, Wesley. "Religion and Science: A New Look at Hume's *Dialogues*."
    Philosophical Studies 33 (1978): 143–176.
Wainwright, William. "The Presence of Evil and the Falsification of Theistic
    Assertions." *Religious Studies* 4 (1969): 213–216.

5

The Problem of
Gratuitous Evil

In the previous chapter, we saw that assessment of probabilities for theism depended not simply on beliefs about evil but also on a larger collection of background beliefs and, ultimately, on one's total evidence set. Since the atheist's total set of beliefs will surely differ from the theist's in important ways, their assignments of probabilities to

(G) An omnipotent, omniscient, wholly good God exists

will differ greatly. For the theist, the probability of (G) is high, whereas for the atheist, it is low. But then it is difficult to see how evil constitutes a probabilistic problem for the *theist*. Additionally, Reformed epistemology's critique of evidentialism, coupled with its perspective on whether evidence is even necessary for one to be rationally entitled to believe (G), forces a reconsideration of the role of atheistic as well as theistic arguments over God's existence.[1] Yet many philosophers—atheists and theists alike—still think that evil provides a basis for some kind of nondeductive or broadly inductive argument against theism. The trick is to arrive at a formulation of an evidential argument from evil that significantly advances the discussion.

Can There Be an Evidential Argument from Evil?

In seeking to determine whether there is some kind of evidential argument that avoids the defects of the logical and probabilistic arguments from evil and still gives some rational basis for not believing in God, we must first remember what defenders have and have not shown. Plantinga has shown that theism is *not improbable* given evil; he has not proved that evil cannot be *evidence against* theistic belief. For example, the testimony of the defendant's husband that she was at home at the time of the murder is evidence against the hypothesis that she is guilty. But the testimony may not show that the hypothesis is improbable if there is enough other evidence of her guilt. Likewise, evils may genuinely be evidence against theism and still not show that the probability of theism is low, if theism is sufficiently probable on other grounds.

Furthermore, Reformed epistemologists point out that the theist may be entirely rational in taking belief in God as basic, that he need not justify it by arguments constructed from other beliefs. However, Reformed epistemology does not entail that evil cannot count as evidence against belief in God. It does undermine unfair efforts to evaluate belief in God probabilistically according to the atheist's own evidential set. More generally, Reformed epistemology calls into question the idea that one is rationally entitled to believe in God only if one has adequate evidence for this belief. None of this, however, shows that evil cannot count against belief in God—even when that belief is construed as basic. The probabilistic problem of evil reflects one (albeit flawed) strategy for showing how evil can be conceived as evidence. It is, then, a potential defeater for theistic belief that itself can be defeated by appropriate defensive maneuvers. But this leaves open the possibility that a more formidable defeater can be fashioned in terms of another type of evidential argument.

Plantinga has clearly shown that the atheistic critic is misguided if he thinks he can produce an argument of coercive force that will compel all reasonable people to agree that theism is improbable with respect to evil and thus that one would not be rational in embracing it. However, it does not follow from this either that atheists have no argument at their disposal regarding the evidential impact of evil on theistic belief or that theists should show no concern for any such argument. The atheistic critic, for instance, may not intend to "coerce" but rather to "persuade" the minds of theists and agnostics. The theist and atheist can reason together about the bearing of evil on the existence of God—as well as the bearing of a great many other things, for that matter—without accusing each other of being irrational or being in violation of some intellectual duties.

Much reasoning in philosophy generally has this persuasive, noncoercive character. Even if it cannot be shown that one position on some controversial issue is more probable than another, it is still legitimate for the position's proponent to make a case for why it is preferable to the other. And it is likewise legitimate for his interlocutor to make a case for his own position, point out weaknesses on the other side, answer objections, and so forth. This all takes on the character of *classical philosophical dialectic*—giving reasons for and against a controversial position. Since such reasoning does sometimes lead to changes of opinion, we may engage in it with a sincere hope of persuading others or of coming to a more adequately justified position ourselves. In the process, we may rely on assessments of plausibility or credibility that are not obvious and not universally accepted. Neither Plantinga's defense against the probabilistic problem nor his presentation of Reformed epistemology has shown that it is useless to offer an evidential problem of evil in this vein. The key is to arrive at some understanding of the kind of nondemonstrative argument that supplies rational grounds for the rejection of theism.

Versions of the Evidential Argument

This kind of nondemonstrative or broadly inductive argument essentially asks the theist to make sense of evil in light of his belief in God. The critic cites some alleged fact about evil as the *evidence* that supports the conclusion that it is more rational, given the evidence, to believe that God does not exist. Three formulations of this kind of argument may be detected in the growing literature on the evidential argument. As with the logical and probabilistic arguments, we may classify these formulations according to which of the following propositions about evil they use:

(E$_1$) Evil exists
(E$_2$) Large amounts, extreme kinds, and perplexing distributions of evil exist
(E$_3$) Gratuitous evil exists.

Thus, we get the taxonomy of arguments shown in Figure 5.1:

FIGURE 5.1   Versions of the Evidential Argument from Evil

IV	V	VI
(E_1) is evidence against (G)	(E_2) is evidence against (G)	(E_3) is evidence against (G)

For each version of the argument, then, a specific (E)-proposition is said to count as evidence against (G).

The first formulation of the evidential argument—Version IV—is not now widely discussed. George Schlesinger, a theist, recognized this version in very early discussions of the evidential argument: "While the question of the amount of evil the world contains most vitally affects our lives, in the context of our problem this is an entirely irrelevant question."[2] According to this version of the argument, any instance of evil at all tends to disconfirm God's existence. However, the critic's hope of making Version IV successful depends on his showing that there is no morally sufficient reason for an omnipotent, omniscient, wholly good God to allow any evil whatsoever. This is a claim that seems well beyond the critic's reach, since a number of thoughtful nontheists admit that some evil serves good ends that could not otherwise be achieved. Therefore, the theist can respond that God, if he exists, could have a morally sufficient reason for allowing *some* evil. The theist might even suggest some general kinds of evils that are connected to some goods (e.g., hardship is connected to character development, danger to heroism, and so forth).

Many critics, however, see Version V as a more promising argument. In *The Faith of a Heretic*, Walter Kaufmann states:

The problem arises when monotheism is enriched with—or impoverished by—two assumptions: that God is omnipotent and that God is just. In fact, popular theism goes beyond merely asserting that God is just and claims that God is "good," that he is morally perfect, that he hates suffering, that he loves man, and that he is infinitely merciful, far transcending all human mercy, love, and perfection. Once these assumptions are granted, the problem arises: why, then, is there *all* the suffering we know? And as long as these assumptions are granted, this question cannot be answered. For if these assumptions were true, it would follow that there could not be all this suffering. Conversely: since it is a fact that there is *all this* suffering, it is plain that at least one of these assumptions must be false. Popular theism is refuted by the existence of *so much* suffering. The theism preached from thousands of pulpits and credited by millions of believers is disproved by Auschwitz and *a billion* lesser evils.[3]

Many theists also acknowledge that this argument is quite formidable. Harvard theologian Gordon Kaufman discusses its force:

> A major stumbling block for contemporary faith in God remains: If there is a God, and if he is loving, why is there such horrendous evil in the world? Do not the facts of terror, pain, and unjustifiable suffering demonstrate either that God is not good—and therefore not worthy of our adoration and worship—or that there is no God at all? . . . Exploration of the *varieties, subtleties,* and *enormities* of evil in human life has become perhaps the principal theme of literature, art, and drama since World War II.[4]

Thus Kaufman admits that

(E2)   Large amounts, extreme kinds, and perplexing distributions of evil exist

can be construed to count against

(G)   An omnipotent, omniscient, wholly good God exists.

Again, it is not the sheer existence of evil per se that counts against the existence of God but the fact that there are so many evils that are very severe and present in patterns defying comprehension.[5]

Formulating a reply to this version of the problem is difficult but not impossible for theists. Some theists have pointed out that this argument rests on an assumption that the theistic deity would allow only certain amounts, kinds, and distributions of evil. Yet it is hard to know how to establish how much evil is *too much* for God to allow. How, in principle, could we establish this? The logic of theism itself does not seem to generate any clear limit on the amount, type, and proportions of evil in the world. It also does not appear that the teachings of Christian theology, which expand upon restricted theism, contain some limit. We could obviously apply one theistic response to Version V here, saying that God could allow quite a lot of evil, even very extreme evil, as long as it serves good purposes that

God could not otherwise achieve. A second question that theists often raise regards how any finite person could ascertain that the present amount of evil in the world far exceeds the divinely set limit. These and other perplexing questions make it difficult to imagine how the atheist could ever establish such claims.[6]

What are we to say, then, about formulation V? In spite of its difficulties, we should not dismiss V too quickly. After all, it is an attempt to articulate one of the deepest and most profound objections to religious disbelief. Expressions of this argument that describe concrete instances of suffering, for example, strike a responsive chord in many thoughtful people, believers and unbelievers alike. The critic can certainly argue strongly that theism fails to explain the large amounts, extreme kinds, and perplexing distributions of evil in the world and that this is a prima facie good reason to reject theism. Further, critics can argue that whatever divine purposes the horrible evils of our world allegedly serve must be shown to be morally worthwhile if God is to be exonerated for permitting them.

The debate over Version V is vigorous and important. Theists typically argue that even quite considerable evil can be allowed by a morally perfect deity as long as it is necessary to either bringing about a greater good or preventing a greater evil. They employ either defenses or theodicies that involve suggestions for what morally sufficient reasons God has or might have along these lines.[7] Atheistic critics find fault in attempts to argue that all evils have a point. But this really brings us to the consideration of the next version of the evidential problem.

Version VI has become a major focus of both atheists and theists alike. We may refer to this version here as the *evidential argument from gratuitous evil*. Many critics who advance Version VI of the evidential argument are willing to admit that the theistic deity might allow vast amounts, extreme kinds, and perplexing distributions of evil to exist. But they insist that God is justified in allowing the magnitude and profusion of evil only if it serves some purpose. Cornman and Lehrer speak of "unnecessary evil," Madden and Hare speak of "gratuitous evil," and Daniel Howard-Snyder speaks of "pointless evil."[8] So, it is gratuitous or pointless evil, if it exists, that provides crucial evidence against the existence of a supremely powerful, wise, and good God. We must now take a look at how the philosophical community has handled this argument from evil.

Analyzing the Evidential Argument from Gratuitous Evil

William Rowe has provided the most widely discussed version of the evidential argument from gratuitous evil. In 1979, Rowe wrote:

(R1)   There exist instances of intense suffering which an omnipotent, omniscient being could have prevented without thereby losing some greater good or permitting some evil equally bad or worse.

(R2)   An omniscient, wholly good being would prevent the occurrence of any intense suffering it could, unless it could not do so without thereby losing some greater good or permitting some evil equally bad or worse.

(R3)   There does not exist an omnipotent, omniscient, wholly good being.[9]

Rowe actually offers a concrete version of this argument by citing a specific instance of intense suffering that could have been prevented without thereby losing some greater good or permitting some evil equally bad or worse. Largely to avoid the Free Will Defense, he describes an instance of natural evil: A helpless fawn is trapped in a forest fire and suffers horribly for days before dying. Now, assuming that premise (R2) is held in common by most theists and atheists, the bulk of the controversy revolves around the first premise.

In providing rational support for premise (R1), Rowe states that the fawn's suffering is "apparently pointless" for "there does not appear to be any outweighing good such that the prevention of the fawn's suffering would require either the loss of that good or the occurrence of an evil equally bad or worse." In later revisions of the argument, Rowe also borrows a case of suffering from Bruce Russell as an instance of moral evil: A five-year-old girl is raped, severely beaten, and strangled to death by her mother's drunken boyfriend. Rowe's two examples are now referred to as "the cases of Bambi and Sue" and employed as two reasons to believe that gratuitous evil exists. Rowe argues, moreover, that even if we could discover that God could not have eliminated these specific cases of seemingly pointless evil without thereby losing some greater good or permitting some evil equally bad or worse, it would still be unreasonable to believe

that all the instances of seemingly pointless human and animal suffering that occur have such a point.[10] Thus, Rowe believes he has provided inductive support for premise (R1).

Rowe's argument has virtually been the paradigm for the evidential
argument from evil since the late 1970s. For present purposes, let us
trim it down as follows:

(R1') Gratuitous evil exists
(R2') If God exists, then gratuitous evil does not exist
(R3') Therefore, God does not exist.

The argument structure here is obviously deductive. The support for
premise (R1') is inductive, making this version of the argument from
evil "evidential."[11]

We must understand *gratuitous evil* (in Rowe's words) as an evil
that an omnipotent, omniscient being could have prevented without
thereby losing some greater good or permitting some evil equally bad
or worse. A gratuitous evil, in this sense, is a state of affairs that is not
necessary (either logically or causally) to the attainment of a greater
good or to the prevention of an evil equally bad or worse. According
to this line of thinking, the only *morally sufficient reason* God can
have for permitting any evil is that it must be necessary either to the
attainment of a greater good or to the prevention of an evil equally
bad or worse.

The Appearance of Evil

Many theists have joined the fray to rebut or mitigate the force of
Rowe's first premise and thus stop the argument from working. Some
of them argue that the instances of apparently pointless evil that
Rowe cites are not generated by following proper inductive tech-
niques, that is, that they are not part of a representative sample.
These theists argue that we are rationally justified in believing that
there are no goods that justify an evil only if we think the goods we
know of are part of a representative sample. Obviously, in making
many ordinary inductive judgments, the range of relevant items in
the sample falls within our range of knowledge (e.g., looking all
around the world and seeing many storks with red legs and then con-
cluding that it is reasonable to believe that all storks have red legs).

But Stephen Wykstra argues that the atheistic critic has no reason to believe that finite human beings can have a representative sample of goods for the sake of which an omnipotent, omniscient, wholly good being would allow evil.

To begin to understand the exact point of this objection to Rowe, we must understand Wykstra's analysis of appears-locutions. He assumes Rowe uses the term "appears" in what Roderick Chisholm calls the "epistemic" sense of the term. That is, it pertains to what we are inclined to believe when we contemplate a situation. Then, Wykstra makes a careful distinction in the different ways that the word "not" functions in such locutions. He argues that Rowe's statement that "there does not appear to be any outweighing good" should not be interpreted as the initial premise in an argument from ignorance, which is a blatant fallacy. Rowe's statement, as Wykstra correctly points out, is better interpreted as meaning that "it appears that there is no outweighing good."[12]

Rowe's inference, then, may be understood as moving from a proposition such as

(42) It appears that some evils are connected to no outweighing goods

to the proposition

(43) It is reasonable to believe that some evils are not connected to outweighing goods.

This reasoning has this general form: (A) It appears that p; therefore, (B) it is reasonable to believe that p.

Such an inference seems warranted by the Principle of Credulity expounded by Richard Swinburne: If something appears to be the case (in the epistemic sense of "appears"), then this prima facie justifies one in believing it is the case.[13] This principle is rooted in a widespread philosophical opinion that we have generally reliable belief-forming powers (e.g., perception, memory) that incline us toward certain beliefs in certain situations.[14] According to Wykstra, however, the Principle of Credulity does not quite provide the criterion we need. He argues that the epistemic relation that the principle posits between (A) and (B) must meet the Condition of Reasonable Epistemic Access (CORNEA):

> CORNEA: On the basis of cognized situation s, human H is entitled to claim "It appears that p" only if it is reasonable for H to believe that, given her cognitive faculties and the use she has made of them, if p were not the case, s would likely be different than it is in some way discernible by her.[15]

In making an appears-claim, one assumes there is an evidential connection between what she is inclined to believe (i.e., that p) and the cognized situation that inclines her to believe it. However, if it is not reasonable for her to believe that this evidential connection obtains, then she is not entitled to say, "It appears that p."

Wykstra argues that applying CORNEA is fatal to Rowe's case, for by CORNEA, one is entitled to claim "this suffering does not appear (i.e., appears not) to serve any Divinely purposed outweighing good" only if it is reasonable to believe that if such a Divinely purposed good exists, it would be within our ken. But it is not reasonable to believe this, according to Wykstra, since an infinitely wise deity would certainly know of outweighing goods that escape our finite understanding. We humans could not expect to know all the goods in virtue of which God permits suffering. They are beyond our ken. Thus, Rowe's claim that there appear to be no outweighing goods for much suffering does not meet the Condition of Reasonable Epistemic Access. If such goods did exist, Wykstra claims that we have no reason to think we would have cognitive access to them.

Wykstra contends that Rowe would have to show that if theism is true, then there is reason to think that we would have access to the all the goods that enter into God's reasons for permitting suffering. Wykstra believes that the prospects for doing this are very bleak. Since he maintains that belief in God's infinite knowledge that exceeds our own is logically implied by theism, the theist should *expect* that we would fail to see outweighing goods for many evils.[16] According to Wykstra, the theist has reason indeed to believe that in many cases of suffering, CORNEA is not met. But then he wonders how Rowe's claim that there appear to be no justifying goods connected to many evils is supposed to be rational support for the key premise that

(R1) There exist instances of intense suffering that an omnipotent, omniscient being could have prevented without thereby losing some greater good or permitting some evil equally bad or worse.

If this premise does not have adequate rational support, that is, if one is not within her epistemic rights to believe it, then it is difficult to see how it can serve as evidence *against* theism.

In replying to Wykstra, Rowe reinforces his position that the fact that various evils "appear" not to have outweighing goods is acceptable rational justification for his premise (R1). He clarifies that his original intention was to discuss *standard theism*, which is the view that there is an omnipotent, omniscient, wholly good being who created the world. Within standard theism, Rowe distinguishes *restricted* theism and *expanded* theism. Restricted theism is strictly the view that the being described by standard theism exists. Expanded theism, however, is the view that this being exists, conjoined with certain other significant religious claims (about sin, redemption, afterlife, and so forth). The essence of Rowe's response to Wykstra, then, is that Wykstra mistakenly defends his own preferred version of expanded theism, whereas Rowe's original attack was mounted against restricted theism. Wykstra's defense, then, misses the point. It might work for his particular version of expanded theism, but it does not help restricted theism at all.

Rowe describes Wykstra's general strategy as an attempt to block his ability to affirm a proposition such as

(44)   It appears that the fawn's suffering is pointless—that is, it appears that the fawn's suffering does not serve an outweighing good otherwise unobtainable by an omnipotent, omniscient being.

Rowe, of course, cites as justification for (44) the fact that we are unable to think of any good that exists or might come into existence that both outweighs the fawn's suffering and could not be obtained by God without permitting that suffering. If this is acceptable support for (44), then the evidential argument from gratuitous evil works.

However, Wykstra counters that Rowe is not entitled to affirm (44) unless the following proposition is true:

(45)   We have no reason to think that were God to exist things would strike us in pretty much the same way concerning the fawn's suffering.

Wykstra's objection focuses, then, on showing (45) to be false by supplying a reason to think that were the fawn's suffering actually to serve an outweighing good, otherwise unobtainable by God, things would still strike us in pretty much the same way—that is, we would be unable to think of any outweighing good for it.

Rowe characterizes Wykstra's reasoning in this way. Wykstra starts with the claim

(46) God's mind grasps goods beyond our ken,

and moves to

(47) It is likely that the goods for the sake of which God permits suffering are, to a large extent, beyond our ken,

and concludes with

(48) It is likely that many of the sufferings in our world do not appear to have a point—we cannot see what goods justify God in permitting them.

For Wykstra, then, proposition (48) is a "logical extension of theism," "implicit" in theism, and not simply an "additional postulate."[17] Armed with a version of theism that includes (48), Wykstra claims that the appearance that many instances of suffering do not have a point is exactly what we would expect if God exists. In other words, (45) is not true.

Rowe agrees that standard theism implies (46) and that it also implies a proposition something like

(49) God allows the sufferings that occur in this world in order to achieve goods he could otherwise not achieve.

But Rowe vigorously disagrees that restricted standard theism implies that these goods, once they occur, remain beyond our ken.[18] That is an implication of some versions of expanded theism, such as Wykstra's, but not of restricted theism itself.

Rowe maintains, then, that Wykstra's move from (46) to (47) is the heart of the difficulty. This move presupposes that the goods in question have not occurred or, if they have occurred, remain unknown to us (in themselves or in their connections to actual sufferings). But restricted standard theism, says Rowe, supplies no reason to think that either of these alternatives is true. Perhaps, prior to their being realized, God's mind grasps goods that we cannot imagine. This much seems deducible from standard theism. But this is no reason to think *either* that the greater goods in virtue of which God permits most sufferings come into existence in the distant future *or* that once they do come into existence, we remain ignorant of them and their relation to the sufferings.[19]

Although restricted standard theism implies that God can apprehend nonactual goods prior to their occurring that lie beyond our ken, this is insufficient to justify Wykstra's claim that, if God were to exist, the sufferings in our world would appear to us as they do. Rowe concludes, therefore, that Wykstra has not supplied a convincing reason to reject his evidential claim:

(R1)   There exist instances of intense suffering that an omnipotent, omniscient being could have prevented without thereby losing some greater good or permitting some evil equally bad or worse.

Thus, for Rowe, a crucial premise in the evidential argument can be shown reasonable to believe, and the argument from gratuitous evil stands.

Notes

1. See Alvin Plantinga, "The Reformed Objection to Natural Theology," *Christian Scholar's Review* 11 (1982): 187–198. See also Nicholas Wolterstorff, "The Migration of the Theistic Arguments: From Natural Theology to Evidentialist Apologetics," in *Rationality, Religious Belief, and Moral Commitment,* eds. Robert Audi and William J. Wainwright (Ithaca: Cornell University Press, 1986), pp. 38–81.

2. George Schlesinger, *Religion and Scientific Method* (Hingham, Mass.: Reidel, 1977), p. 13.

3. Walter Kaufmann, *The Faith of a Heretic* (Garden City, N.Y.: Doubleday, 1961), p. 139 (italics mine).

4. Gordon D. Kaufman, *God: The Problem* (Cambridge, Mass.: Harvard University, 1972), pp. 171–172 (italics mine).

5. Paul Draper has offered the most sophisticated recent rendition of argument V in "Pain and Pleasure: An Evidential Problem for Theists," in *The Evidential Argument from Evil,* ed. Daniel Howard-Snyder (Bloomington: Indiana University Press, 1996), pp. 12–29. In the early 1980s, I introduced

the language of "amount," "kind," and "distribution" into the discussion of the evidential argument in my *Evil and the Christian God* (Grand Rapids, Mich.: Baker Book House, 1982), p. 67. Peter van Inwagen has more recently used these concepts as the basis for an article on the problem of evil. See his "The Magnitude, Duration, and Distribution of Evil: A Theodicy," *Philosophical Perspectives* 5 (1991): 135–165. Bruce Russell acknowledges this kind of problem in "Defenseless," in *The Evidential Argument from Evil*, ed. Daniel Howard-Snyder (Bloomington: Indiana University Press, 1996), pp. 194, 199ff.

6. Peter van Inwagen discusses the difficulties surrounding the argument over the amount and kinds of evil in his "The Problem of Evil, the Problem of Air, and the Problem of Silence," *Philosophical Perspectives* 5 (1991): 135–165, especially pp. 140–152.

7. Such an appraisal of the situation seems more intellectually honest and more philosophically promising than denying that there really is as much evil or that multitudes of people are really as unhappy as is initially supposed. It is better for the theist simply to admit that there are a great many severe evils in the world and then to argue that the existence of God is neither precluded nor made unlikely thereby. The argument can be constructed either from the logic of essential theistic concepts or from the additional concepts included in some expanded form of theism that is represented in a living faith tradition, such as Christianity.

Although such theistic maneuvers seem reasonable, perhaps there is at least one sense in which the evidential argument from the amounts, kinds, and distribution of evil is immediately destructive to religious belief. The argument clearly discredits belief in a deity who places a felicitous limitation on the evils that human beings can experience and about whom simplistic answers for evil may be given. Thus, the god of popular folk religion—often peddled in the name of historical, orthodox Christianity—really is dead. The burden, then, falls upon the shoulders of thoughtful Christian theists to articulate a concept of God that is more sophisticated and profound than popular theism envisions.

8. J. W. Cornman and Keith Lehrer, *Philosophical Problems and Arguments: An Introduction* (New York: Macmillan, 1970), p. 347; Edward Madden and Peter Hare, *Evil and the Concept of God* (Springfield, Ill.: Charles C. Thomas, 1968), p. 3; Daniel Howard-Snyder, "The Argument from Inscrutable Evil," in his *Evidential Argument from Evil* (Bloomington: Indiana University Press, 1996), pp. 291–292.

9. William Rowe, "The Problem of Evil and Some Varieties of Atheism," *American Philosophical Quarterly* 16 (1979): 336. I have changed numbers and added parentheses to Rowe's argument in keeping with the convention for numbering used throughout this book.

10. Ibid., p. 337.

11. In terms we used earlier,

(E₃) Gratuitous evil exists

counts as negative evidence against

(G) An omnipotent, omniscient, wholly good God exists.

But what is the significant negative evidential relationship to (G) in which (E₃) stands? Bruce Russell explains that there are really two ways of conceiving of this evidential relationship, one *inductive* and the other *abductive*. Although we cannot pursue this distinction here, the reader is encouraged to read Russell's "Defenseless," pp. 193–218.

12. Stephen Wykstra, "The Humean Obstacle to Evidential Arguments from Suffering: On Avoiding the Evils of 'Appearance,'" *International Journal for Philosophy of Religion* 16 (1984): 80–81.

13. Richard Swinburne, *The Existence of God* (Oxford: Clarendon Press, 1979), pp. 245, 254.

14. For example, Swinburne cites an example of a belief formed on the basis of sensory experience: "If I say 'the ship appears to be moving' I am saying that I am inclined to believe that the ship is moving, and that it is my present sensory experience which leads me to have this inclination to belief." See his *Existence of God*, p. 246. For a fuller discussion of these cognitive powers and their function, see Alvin Plantinga, *Warrant and Proper Function* (New York: Oxford University Press, 1993).

15. Wykstra, "Humean Obstacle," p. 85.

16. Ibid., p. 89.

17. Ibid., pp. 89, 91.

18. William Rowe, "Evil and the Theistic Hypothesis: A Response to Wykstra," *International Journal for Philosophy of Religion* 16 (1984): 99.

19. Rowe observes that we could, of course, imagine a version of expanded theism that conjoins a proposition such as

The goods for the sake of which God must permit suffering will be realized only at the end of the world

with standard theism. This version of expanded theism is not rendered unlikely by the items that render restricted theism unlikely. See ibid.

Suggested Readings

Alston, William. "The Inductive Argument from Evil and the Human Cognitive Condition." *Philosophical Perspectives* 5 (1991): 29–67.

Beaty, Michael D. "The Problem of Evil: The Unanswered Questions Argument." *Southwest Philosophy Review* 4 (1988): 57–64.

Chrzan, Keith. "Necessary Gratuitous Evil: An Oxymoron Revisited." *Faith and Philosophy* 11 (1994): 134–137.

_____. "When Is a Gratuitous Evil Really Gratuitous?" *International Journal for Philosophy of Religion* 24 (1988): 87–91.

Dore, Clement. "Does Suffering Serve Valuable Ends?" In *Theism.* Dordrecht: D. Reidel, 1984.

Feinberg, John S. *The Many Faces of Evil: Theological Systems and the Problem of Evil.* 2nd ed. Grand Rapids, Mich.: Zondervan, 1994.

Geach, Peter. *Providence and Evil.* Cambridge: Cambridge University Press, 1977.

Hasker, William. "Chrzan on Necessary Gratuitous Evil." *Faith and Philosophy* 12 (1995): 423–425.

_____. "The Necessity of Gratuitous Evil." *Faith and Philosophy* 9 (1992): 23–44.

_____. "Providence and Evil: Three Theories." *Religious Studies* 28 (1992): 91–105.

Hick, John. *Evil and the God of Love.* 2nd ed. New York: Harper & Row, 1978.

Howard-Snyder, Daniel. *The Evidential Argument from Evil.* Bloomington: Indiana University Press, 1996.

_____. "Seeing Through CORNEA." *International Journal for Philosophy of Religion* 32 (1992): 25–49.

Madden, Edward, and Peter Hare. "Evil and Inconclusiveness." *Sophia (Australia)* 11 (January-June 1972): 8–12.

O'Connor, David. "Hasker on Necessary Gratuitous Evil." *Faith and Philosophy* 12 (1995): 380–392.

Peterson, Michael. *Evil and the Christian God.* Grand Rapids, Mich.: Baker Book House, 1982.

_____. "God and Evil in Process Theology." In *Process Theology*, edited by Ronald Nash. Grand Rapids, Mich.: Baker Book House, 1987, pp. 117–139.

_____. "God and Evil: Problems of Consistency and Gratuity." *Journal of Value Inquiry* 13 (1979): 305–313.

_____. "Recent Work on the Problem of Evil." *American Philosophical Quarterly* 20 (1983): 321–339.

Peterson, Michael, ed. *The Problem of Evil: Selected Readings.* Notre Dame, Ind.: University of Notre Dame Press, 1992.

Peterson, Michael, William Hasker, Bruce Reichenbach, and David Basinger. *Reason and Religious Belief: An Introduction to the Philosophy of Religion.* 2nd ed. New York: Oxford University Press, 1998, chap. 6, pp. 116–145.

Rowe, William L. "The Empirical Argument from Evil." In *Rationality, Religious Belief, and Moral Commitment,* edited by Robert Audi and William Wainwright. Ithaca: Cornell University Press, 1986, pp. 227–247.

_____. "Evil and Theodicy." *Philosophical Topics* 16 (Fall 1988): 119–132.

_____. "Evil and the Theistic Hypothesis: A Response to S. J. Wykstra." *International Journal for Philosophy of Religion* 16 (1984): 95–100.

_____. "The Problem of Evil." In *Philosophy of Religion: An Introduction*. Encino and Belmont, Calif.: Dickenson, 1978, pp. 79–95.

_____. "The Problem of Evil and Some Varieties of Atheism." *American Philosophical Quarterly* 16 (1979): 335–341.

_____. "Ruminations About Evil." *Philosophical Perspectives* 5 (1991): 69–88.

Russell, Bruce. "The Persistent Problem of Evil." *Faith and Philosophy* 6 (1989): 121–139.

Russell, Bruce, and Stephen Wykstra. "The 'Inductive' Argument from Evil: A Dialogue." *Philosophical Topics* 16 (Fall 1988): 133–160.

Sennett, James F. "The Inscrutable Evil Defense." *Faith and Philosophy* 10 (1993): 220–229.

Stewart, Melville. *The Greater-Good Defense: An Essay on the Rationality of Faith*. New York: St. Martin's, 1993.

Trau, Jane Mary. "Fallacies in the Argument from Gratuitous Suffering." *The New Scholasticism* 60 (1986): 585–589.

van Inwagen, Peter. "The Magnitude, Duration, and Distribution of Evil: A Theodicy." *Philosophical Topics* 16 (Fall 1988): 161–187.

_____. "The Place of Chance in a World Sustained by God." In *Divine and Human Action*, edited by Thomas V. Morris. Ithaca: Cornell University Press, 1988, pp. 211–235.

_____. "The Problem of Evil, the Problem of Air, and the Problem of Silence." *Philosophical Perspectives* 5 (1991): 135–165.

6

The Task of Theodicy

The evidential argument from gratuitous evil is now widely considered the most formidable objection to theistic belief. Clearly, *defense* against this as well as other objections from evil is an important type of theistic response. Yet many classical and contemporary theists have responded in an altogether different mode. These theists engage in what has traditionally been called *theodicy.* The term derives from the Greek *theos* (god) and *dikē* (justice) and is, as John Milton says, an attempt to "justify the ways of God to man." Rather than propose *merely possible* reasons God might have for permitting evil, a theodicy seeks to articulate *plausible* or *credible explanations* that rest on theistic truths and insights. Just as contemporary analytic philosophers of religion have sharply distinguished the logical and evidential problems of evil, they also have carefully defined the strategic functions of defense and theodicy. Although debate about the viability of theodicy continues, many interesting and influential theodicies have been advanced in the discussion of God and evil. I review here discussions of the feasibility of theodicy. Then, I will take a close look at four famous theodicies, from Augustine, Gottfried Leibniz, John Hick, and Alfred North Whitehead.

The Prospects for Theodicy

Most theistic responses to the argument from gratuitous evil revolve around its factual premise, which is the claim that there is (or probably is) gratuitous evil. William Rowe writes: "If we are to fault this argument, . . . we must find some fault with its [factual] premise."[1] Madden and Hare state that "the really interesting problem of evil is whether the apparent gratuity can be explained away . . . or whether the gratuity [of evil] is real and hence detrimental to religious belief."[2] Keith Yandell, a theist, insists that "the crucial question is whether it is certain, or at least more probable than not, that there is unjustified evil, whether natural or moral."[3] Almost all defenses as well as theodicies based on standard theism react to the factual premise of the argument.

Theistic defenses against the factual claim that there is gratuitous evil—such as Wykstra's, Alston's, and van Inwagen's[4]—typically cite the severe cognitive limitations of human beings in relation to divine wisdom. According to these theists, such limitations bar the critic from claiming that it is reasonable to believe that there are no offsetting goods connected to many evils in the world. The goods that justify God in allowing evil are, they contend, beyond our ken, known to the divine mind but not to our minds. Because of these same cognitive limitations, many theists who offer a defense declare theodicy to be impossible or unnecessary or inappropriate. Some see theodicy as impossible because it requires knowing the reasons for evil that only the divine wisdom can know. Even if it were not strictly impossible to know God's reasons for evil, others would argue that theodicy would still be unnecessary because it exceeds what pure defense coupled with Reformed epistemology requires of the theist in the debate with the critic. Some even say that theodicy is inappropriate because it displays the presumption and arrogance of mere humans trying to probe into divine mysteries. Let us look at each of these objections in turn.

A great many Christian theists, past and present, have not considered theodicy impossible. Most of them have not thought that formulating a theodicy requires knowing God's reasons for evil as though finite human beings could completely fathom the infinite divine wisdom. Rather, they conceive of the project of theodicy as drawing out the implications of one's theological position for evil. After all, religious believers commonly accept that the doctrines and teachings of their faith have implications for all sorts of important matters—moral and spiritual virtues, the meaning of redemption, the purpose of human life, and so forth. So, it would be odd indeed to think that religious beliefs have no implications whatsoever for understanding something so important as evil in the world. In a sense, then, Christian theism already contains implicit theodical insights that may be made explicit and systematic. In fact, some Christian traditions forthrightly claim that it is God's good pleasure to give us at least dim and partial glimpses of his general purposes, including his purposes for evil. (Here we simply have to recognize differences among Christian traditions or what we are calling versions of expanded theism, and some are more positive toward theodicy.) Whatever degree of understanding of evil that believers achieve, then, provides a measure of theodicy. Thus, theodicy is not impossible.

Not all theists agree with what we might call the Reformed objection to theodicy, which designates defense as the theist's only responsibility in the debate with the critic and offers a theory of how belief in God can be epistemically basic. Yet developing a theodicy seems completely justified to theists who construe the dialectical context of rational debate in a certain fashion. The theist might see himself not as asserting the isolated claim that "God exists" but rather as asserting a whole set of logically interrelated claims regarding the divine nature and purposes. He might even understand the single claim "God exists" to be invested with this larger interpretive scheme and therefore entailing all sorts of other claims about God's ways with the world. He could maintain that the whole system of beliefs that constitute his understanding of theism offers an interpretation of human life and the world at large. The dialectic develops, then, when the critic alleges that this theological interpretation has difficulty accounting for evil. The theist responds by trying to elucidate and explain how his theological beliefs make sense of evil. Here the critic is not being eccentric or unfair to request that the theist make sense of his own belief in God, particularly by tracing out its ramifications for the issue of evil. So, when the context of dialogue is conceived differently, theodicy is not unnecessary.

Even if we grant that the believer may be entitled to accept belief in God as basic under certain conditions, it is naive to think that life's experiences will never invite deeper reflection upon that belief, reflection that includes questioning as well as reaffirming one's faith. When engaging in this kind of honest reflection, thoughtful believers explore the implications of their unique particular Christian and theistic perspective for a large number of important issues—moral crises, the worth of certain humanitarian projects, the hope of life after death, and the presence of evil. Thus, it is quite legitimate for theists to try to formulate some reasonable understanding of evil for themselves, and whatever understanding they obtain moves them in the direction of theodicy. This activity need not be characterized as exhibiting the haughty presumption that a finite human being can know the divine mind. Instead, it may be seen as the process of "faith seeking understanding" (*fides quaerens in-tellectum*). Hence, theodicy is not inappropriate.

If theodicy is not impossible or unnecessary or inappropriate, then the way is open to discuss a variety of issues at the level of *metatheod-icy*. For example, how much conceptual work can or ought theodicy accomplish? That is, can theodicy specify God's reason for allowing particular evils? Or should it aim at explaining why God allows the broad kinds of evils that exist? Must a theodicy rest on just one theme (e.g., punishment or character building)? Or can it weave together several themes and insights into an overall picture of the sort of world God created and sustains? And what role does our particular moral theory play in the creation of theodicy? What difference does it make, say, whether we adopt a consequentialist or a deontological moral theory? Where are appropriate building blocks for theodicy to be found—in restricted theism or in some version of expanded theism? How these and many more related questions are settled determines the direction theodicy will take.

Without attempting to discuss these questions in detail, let us say that all of the theodicies considered here try to give some highly general explanations for the evils we find in our world. Furthermore, since restricted theism provides very little material for theodicy, each of the following theodicies relies on some form of expanded theism adopted by the theodicist. In developing their theodicies, Christian theists extract themes from the Bible and historical church teachings as well as insights prevalent in the community of believers, thus tapping into a rich vein of ideas. Of course, various Christian traditions will yield different forms of expanded theism. The theodicist then reflects upon the various ideas available within his tradition and construes them in a way that accounts for evil in the world.

The motivation for theodicy, of course, is that we do not readily see the purpose of much evil. Without at least a general account of evil from a theistic perspective, then, evil appears pointless. Hence, we have the force of Rowe's first premise:

(R1)   There exist instances of intense suffering that an omni-potent, omniscient being could have prevented without thereby losing some greater good or permitting some evil equally bad or worse.

Most theodicies therefore follow the strategy of specifying either greater goods that are gained or worse evils that are averted by God's permitting evil.[5] We may call this general approach "Greater-Good Theodicy." Greater-Good Theodicy is, so to speak, the "parent," and many particular theodicies are its "offspring."[6] The various offspring theodicies may specify different offsetting goods for the evils of the world, but they all agree in assuming that the justification of God consists in specifying some greater good.[7] The difference between a Greater-Good Defense and a Greater-Good Theodicy, of course, is that the former claims it is *possible* that some proposed greater good justifies evil whereas the latter claims that the proposed good *in fact* justifies evil.

Augustine's Free Will Theodicy

The first fully formed theodicy in the Western world was offered by St. Augustine, an early Christian philosopher and theologian. In part, Augustine was rebutting Manichaean Dualism, which holds that two equal cosmic powers, one Good and the other Evil, are at war in the universe. For Manichaeism, the Good power, which people worship, is therefore not absolute. For Augustine, however, the Christian worldview entails that God is absolutely sovereign over all things and that no evil comes from him. So, Augustine undertook the task of showing how the disturbing and undeniable presence of evil in no way detracts from God's total sovereignty.

Augustine offers a comprehensive vision of reality that brings together several strands of thought. One of Augustine's central ideas is that God is supreme in reality and goodness. He also believes that the universe—that is, the whole of God's creation—is good. Only God has the power to bestow being upon finite creatures, and God only creates good things. All of the creatures in God's creation, then, are good in their essence. Augustine embraces a recurring theme in Western philosophy: the linkage of being and goodness. Here we must understand "being" not as bare "existence" (which does not admit of degrees) but as having more or less "intensity" (in the sense, say, that a poetic genius lives more intensely than a simpleton). Intensity admits of degrees. In Augustine's terminology, everything has some degree of "measure, form, and order,"[8] which is its proportion of being. Just as God's being is infinite and absolute, so his goodness is infinite and unsurpassable. God's creation is rich and variegated, filled with all levels of being, and the goodness of all things is correlated to the degree of measure, form, and order he has given them. On the scale of created things, an artichoke is more valuable than a rock, a gorilla is more valuable than an artichoke, and a human being is more valuable than a gorilla—all because of their relative degrees of being.[9]

Evil, then, from Augustine's perspective, is not a thing, not a being. Although evil in human experience can be very powerful and profound, evil does not, at least metaphysically speaking, represent the positive existence of anything. Evil simply does not exist in its own right; it is not one of the constituents of the universe. Rather, it is the lack of reality and thus the lack of goodness. Put another way, evil enters creation when created beings cease to function as they were created to function by nature. Evil is thus metaphysical deprivation, privation, or degradation. Augustine's term for evil is *privatio boni* (privation of good).

For Augustine, evil enters creation through the misuse of finite free will. He attributes all evils, both natural and moral, to the wrong choices of free rational beings. This evil choice is "sin" in theological language. Augustine's interpretation of Christian teachings leads him to assert that, first, a company of angels (nonembodied rational free beings) rebelled against God and that this rebellion was then replicated in humankind (embodied rational free beings). In order to explain how free rational creatures—which represent a very valuable kind of being—can fall away from God, Augustine appeals to the classic Christian doctrine of "creation out of nothing" (*creatio ex nihilo*). Since creatures are brought into being "out of nothing," they are "mutable" or changeable. Only God, the Creator, is "immutable" or unchangeable. So, although the finite rational creature is originally good, it has the capability for sin.

This line of thought clearly gives rise to the unavoidable dilemma of accounting for how an unqualifiedly good creature can commit sin. On the one hand, if the creature is perfect according to its place in the scale of being, then it is difficult to envision how it would commit sin. On the other hand, if the creature is initially flawed and thus commits sin, it is difficult to see how to exonerate God of blame. This dilemma arises with regard to human creatures; it arises with respect to angelic creatures as well. Friedrich Schleiermacher pressed the point: "The more perfect these good angels are supposed to have been, the less possible it is to find any motive but those presupposing a fall already, e.g., arrogance and envy."[10] Unable to find a satisfactory logical solution to this difficulty, Augustine eventually retreats into the "mystery of finite freedom." Somehow, the free, originally good creature originated an evil act. That is a great "mystery."

Of course, the classic Christian belief in God's omniscience entails that God knew before the act of creation that the creature would sin. So, God bears the ultimate responsibility for the creation of beings that he knew would, if created, freely fall into sin. Augustine addresses divine responsibility in creation by developing a conception of sovereign predestination. In Adam, the whole human race sinned, since the race was "seminally present" in his loins.[11] Thus, all of humankind is guilty of sin and subject to condemnation. Yet in God's sovereign grace, which is to us a mystery, some are predestined to salvation while the rest of humanity is allowed to receive its just punishment: "God leads some in mercy and repentance, and others in just judgment does not lead."[12] The sovereign election of some to salvation is due to God's mercy, not to their own merits. Thus, Augustine subsumes the mystery of free will under the mystery of predestination. Of course, many important questions deserve more thorough discussion than I can provide here—for example, whether the concept of free will needed to fit with concepts of divine foreknowledge and predestination is adequate to the reality of significant human freedom, whether a moral critique of God's apparent arbitrariness in predestination is devastating, and so on. At this point, however, I must be content with laying out a few more important themes in Augustinian theodicy and then evaluating it in light of the concerns of this book.

The larger perspective of Augustinian theodicy is not complete without including what Arthur Lovejoy calls "the principle of plentitude."[13] This theme, which held sway in Western intellectual history from Plato to Leibniz, envisions the whole universe as a complex and variegated order of different kinds of created beings, from least to greatest, each kind exhibiting its own unique qualities as well as limitations. In the hands of Augustine, this metaphysical interpretation assumes that God knows that it is good to fill every level of creation, up and down the scale, with finite beings, making creation rich and full. The principle of plentitude helps to account for what we call "evil" due to creaturely finitude.

Perhaps the final key that makes Augustinian theodicy fall into place is what John Hick calls the "aesthetic theme."[14] This is the assumption that the whole of creation, even including those aspects we call evil, is good when seen from God's perspective. Related, of course, to the idea of the universe as a graded diversity, the aesthetic theme is used by Augustine to stress the "beauty" and "fitness" of the universe seen as a whole. So, the uniqueness of each grade or kind of finite creature is somehow complementary in an overall scheme that is harmonious, beautiful, and balanced in the sight of God. The determinate characteristics of each kind of creature, then, betoken its place in the great chain of being (e.g., the swiftness of the cheetah, the beauty of a giant sequoia), as do its limitations (e.g., the pig is not as beautiful as the peacock, the dog does not live as long as the elephant).

It may seem that the aesthetic emphasis here explains natural evil better than it does moral evil. Yet Augustine obviously extends it to cover moral evil by reference to justly deserved, properly proportioned punishment that settles accounts for wrongs that were done. Augustine sees even the fall of the human race and the damnation of sinners as subsumed under the "perfection" and "beauty" of the universe.[15] He states: "For as the beauty of a picture is increased by well-managed shadows, so, to the eye that has skill to discern it, the universe is beautified even by sinners, though, considered by themselves, their deformity is a sad blemish."[16] The result of pressing the aesthetic theme to the fullest is that everything in God's creation contributes to the beauty and appropriateness of the whole—even natural and moral evil.[17] "If it were not good that evil things exist, they would certainly not be allowed to exist by the Omnipotent Good."[18]

Clearly, the upshot of Augustinian theodicy is the denial of the factual premise of the argument from gratuitous evil. Everything in the universe serves the higher harmony of God's sovereign design. There is no state of affairs without which the universe would have been better: "God judged it better to bring good out of evil than not to permit any evil to exist."[19] All evil serves a greater good.

Leibniz's Best Possible World Theodicy

Gottfried Wilhelm von Leibniz (1646–1716) is the only thinker included in the present study who has written a book explicitly entitled *Theodicy*.[20] Leibnizian theodicy seeks to demonstrate that God cannot be blamed for the existence of evil in the world, since this world is the best of all possible worlds. Leibniz's argument utilizes the concept of a "possible world" that was introduced in Chapter 3. Technically speaking, a *possible world* is a total possible state of affairs, a complete universe with past, present, and future. Possibility here, as defined in Chapter 2, is broadly logical possibility. For Leibniz, God's omnipotence ensures that God has the power to actualize any possible world he chooses from among an infinite number of eternally fixed possibilities. God's perfect goodness, which always and unerringly acts for the best, ensures that he will choose to create the most valuable possible world. And God's omniscience ensures that he understands all possible worlds that he could create, accurately calculates their worth, and identifies the very best one. So, the theistic concept of God entails the conclusion that whatever world exists is indeed the best of all possible ones.

Of course, no creaturely reality can be totally perfect, and at least in that sense, reality will contain some evil (i.e., "metaphysical evil").[21] According to Leibniz, God's goodness and power guarantee that he will select that possible world from among all other alternatives that contains the optimum balance of good and evil. Some interpreters of Leibniz mistakenly think he maintains that God brought about that world containing the least amount of evil commensurate with there being a world at all. However, a more correct interpretation of Leibniz is that he envisions God actualizing that possible world that contains the amount of evil necessary to make the world the best one on the whole. And frankly, this may not mean actualizing the world that has the least amount of evil. It may mean bringing about a world that has a great many evils in it but evils of such kinds and arranged in such ways that they contribute to the world being the very best one possible. As Leibniz says, the actual world contains those possible states of affairs "which, being united, produce most reality, most perfection, most significance."[22] Sometimes he employs an aesthetic motif, reminiscent of Augustine, indicating that mere quantitative maximalization is dull and uninteresting, that God seeks to produce richness and quality in the world.

In the process of comparing and evaluating all possible worlds, God foresees the natural and moral evil they contain. He chooses to actualize that world whose various constituents—even its evil constituents—make it the best on the whole: "Not only does [God] derive from [evils] greater goods, but he finds them connected with the greatest goods of all those that are possible: so that it would be a fault not to permit them."[23] Simply put, all the evils of the world contribute to its character as the best of all possible worlds: "If the smallest evil that comes to pass in the world were missing in it, it would no longer be this world; which, with nothing omitted and all allowance made, was found the best by the Creator who chose it."[24]

There are many points of serious philosophical interest in Leibniz's theodicy—for example, its conception of the relation between divine omnipotence and human free will,[25] the standard of value according to which this possible world is the "best," and the prospect that it impugns God's power that he cannot make a better world than this one. Yet the point of central interest for us is this theodicy's bearing on the factual premise of the argument from gratuitous evil. Leibnizian theodicy is tantamount to a denial of the factual premise. The evil that exists is indispensable to the value of the universe considered as a whole. Leibniz's argument is not an empirical one that starts with the evils that actually exist in the world and argues that they contribute to the best value of the whole. Instead, the argument starts with several crucial assumptions about God's attributes and purposes, which are taken as axiomatic and which yield a demonstration that this world must be the best one possible. It is a world that contains no gratuitous evil.

Hick's Soul-Making Theodicy

Although St. Anselm, St. Thomas Aquinas, Leibniz, and other traditional thinkers may be seen as following in the broad Augustinian tradition in theodicy, there is another major approach to theodicy that also has roots in Christian antiquity. This type of theodicy can be traced to Bishop Irenaeus (c. 130–c. 202). The most articulate contemporary proponent of Irenaean theodicy is John Hick, and it is his presentation that we will examine. The main difference between the two traditions may be plainly put: Augustinian theodicy looks back to the fall of a good creation through the misuse of human freedom; Irenaean theodicy looks to the future in terms of God's plan for the development of humanity. However, the ostensible aim of Irenaean theodicy is the same as that of Augustinian theodicy: to relieve God of responsibility for evil.

According to Hick, Adam, the first human, and the rest of the original creation were innocent and immature, possessing the privilege of becoming good by loving God and fellow creatures. But it would be an error to hold, as Augustinian theodicy does, that original innocence can be equated with original perfection. Indeed, it is not at all clear that God can instantaneously create morally mature persons, since moral maturity almost certainly requires struggling, grappling with temptation over time, and probably participating in evil. But even if God could create by fiat a morally mature human person, Hick says, "one who has attained to goodness by meeting and eventually mastering temptations, and thus by rightly making responsible choices in concrete situations, is good in a richer and more valuable sense than would be one created *ab initio* in a state either of innocence or of virtue."[26] Hence, evil as we know it is explained not as a decline from a state of pristine purity and goodness but rather as an inevitable stage in the gradual growth and struggle of the human race. Hick also states: "I suggest . . . that it is an ethically reasonable judgement, even though in the nature of the case not one that is capable of demonstrative proof, that human goodness slowly built up through personal histories of moral effort has a value in the eyes of the Creator which justifies even the long travail of the soul-making process."[27] Thus, humanity was not created perfect but is in the process of being perfected.

Hick labels his Irenaean-type approach *soul-making theodicy* because it paints a picture of God's grand scheme of helping relatively immature human beings become morally and spiritually mature. The world we inhabit is an environment designed to promote God's plan of soul-making. An environment conducive to personal growth must be one in which there are real challenges, real opportunities for the display of moral virtue, and real possibilities for expressing faith in God. A major component of this environment is a community of moral agents who interact in a variety of special ways—deciding on the kinds of relationships they will have, what projects they will pursue, and how they will live together. Another component is a physical order of impersonal objects that operate independent of our wills: atoms and molecules, fields of energy, ocean currents, biological cells, and innumerable other physical things. Obviously, in this kind of environment, there are opportunities to develop moral character as well as distinctively spiritual qualities. Equally obviously, in such conditions there is the genuine risk of evil—of failure and ruin, suffering and injustice.

Interestingly, Hick even deems it important that the world appear as if there is no God, and evil certainly plays an important role in forming this appearance. For Hick, the potentially atheistic appearance of the world creates "epistemic distance" between creature and Creator.[28] He thinks that, if the presence of God were impressed too forcefully upon human consciousness, people would readily acknowledge that God exists and authentic faith would not be possible. So, God has to conceal his presence from us, having an important dual effect. On the one hand, epistemic distance has the effect of making it virtually inevitable that human beings will organize their lives apart from God and in self-centered competition with their fellow human beings. Thus, our state of fallenness represents the way we humans were made, not a descent from a prior state of holiness. On the other hand, epistemic distance has the result of making room for sincere, uncompelled acceptance of God's gracious invitation to a life of faith and trust.[29]

Within the general framework of an Irenaean vision of soul-making, Hick faces the realities of evil and suffering in human life. In regard to moral evil, Hick says that the possibility of wrong choice and action is necessary to the kind of world that is conducive to personal growth. He is willing to agree with Mackie, Flew, and others that it is *logically possible* that God could have created free finite beings who always do what is morally right. But then he emphasizes that the spiritual dimension requires the freedom either to reject God or to come to him: "According to Christianity, the divine purpose for men is not only that they shall freely act rightly towards one another but that they shall also freely enter into a filial personal relationship with God Himself. There is, in other words, a religious as well as an ethical dimension to this purpose."[30] It is relationship with God, then, that makes it *logically impossible* for God to have so constituted humans that they freely respond to him, manifesting love and trust and faith. So, Hick's argument is that God created the world with the possibility of moral evil (or sin, from a theological perspective) as the kind of environment in which humans could exercise authentic faith in him as well as manifest love and virtue toward their fellows.

In regard to pain and suffering, Hick argues that it is rational to recognize the value of a world of physical objects operating by stable natural laws. In such a world, both pleasure and pain are possible for the sentient creatures inhabiting it. But he turns this feature of the world into fodder for his soul-building thesis, explaining that a pain-free, soft, unchallenging world would be inhabited by a soft, unchallenged race of free beings. Hick then distinguishes "suffering" (as a qualitatively unique psychic state) from "pain" (as a physical state). Though pain may sometimes be the source of suffering, it is not always or even usually so. Suffering is a distinct and very profound human phenomenon.

Hick defines suffering as "that state of mind in which we wish violently or obsessively that our situation were otherwise." This state of mind can be as complex and high-level as the human mind itself—related to regret and remorse, to anxiety and despair, to guilt and shame, or to the loss of a loved one. Even what makes, say, a terminal illness produce suffering is not only the physical pain involved but the anticipation of loss. Now, suffering or anguish is usually self-regarding in focus but is sometimes other-regarding. Hick attributes suffering to sin and its consequences for our improper attitudes toward our own finitude, weakness, and mortality. Sin keeps us from being fully conscious of God and humbly and joyfully accepting his universal purposes for good. Again, just as physical pain is an ingredient of a world in which the soul-building purposes of God can be carried out, so suffering is also a feature of such a world. It prompts human beings to search for the deeper meanings of their existence, helping prepare them for mutual service to each other amid suffering and for turning to God.

Much of Hick's argument revolves around the instrumental (teleological) value of the evils of this world: Both natural and moral evils contribute to the soul-making process. Hick assumes that he has won the point that a hedonistic paradise—or at least a world without significant challenge and opportunity—does not contribute to solid moral character or authentic religious faith. It seems that a considerable amount of many kinds of evils would be necessary to any world that could be an environment for soul-making. Whatever amounts and kinds are necessary, then, are not gratuitous but justified in the sense we have been discussing. At this point, it appears that Hick is ready to deny the factual premise of the argument from gratuitous evil, since he has obviously identified much evil that serves a good purpose.

But then Hick asks the haunting question regarding why God allows "dysteleological evil," that is, those evils that are excessive and go beyond anything rationally required of a soul-making process:

> Need the world contain the more extreme and crushing evils which it in fact contains? Are not life's challenges often so severe as to be self-defeating when considered as soul-making influences? Man must (let us suppose) cultivate the soil so as to win his bread by the sweat of his brow; but need there be the gigantic famines, for example in China, from which millions have so miserably perished?[31]

Hick states that it would have been better if such events had never happened,[32] an admission that seems to embrace the fact of gratuitous evil. Then he moves on to ask how, from the standpoint of Christian theodicy, we can address the utterly destructive evils in our world. Why does this world seem less like an environment for soul-building and more like a cold and indifferent, if not outright hostile and malevolent, place?[33]

Hick ultimately says that the excess and random character of much evil is mysterious to us. We see no constructive purpose for it. But then he begins to bring even dysteleological or excessive evil within the ambit of soul-making theodicy, saying that even the mystery of dysteleological evil has soul-making value. He argues that the human misery in this world calls forth deep personal sympathy and energetic efforts to help.[34] He contends that unless the suffering is really undeserved and actually bad for the sufferer, we would not have such desirable and valuable passionate reactions. He also argues that, in a world where suffering and prosperity were exactly proportioned to desert, we would lose the moral environment in which persons do what is right simply for the sake of what is right. Instead, persons would act prudentially so as to bring about the most favorable consequences for themselves. So, by the end of his treatment of dysteleological evil, it is not clear that the evil remains dysteleological. In the end, there is no gratuitous evil for Hick because all evil serves a purpose. He says that God permits evil to "bring out of it an even greater good than would have been possible if evil had never existed."[35]

A study of Hick's Irenaean version of theodicy would not be complete without analyzing his view of life after death as the continuation of God's plan of soul-making. Hick argues that God's plan is the universal salvation of all persons, a process that extends beyond earthly existence and into the afterlife. For those people who, for whatever reasons, depart mortal life without having achieved the proper degree of moral and spiritual maturity (or soul-hood, one might say), God pursues his same objective for them in the life to come. After all, some of these persons would have been among those who suffered terribly and whose lives were snuffed out without a fair chance to mature along moral and spiritual lines. So, God continues his efforts in the afterlife, providing occasions for exercising love and trust, until all persons are brought into the heavenly kingdom. He notes that the universal salvation of humanity is not a logical necessity within Irenaean theology but is a "practical certainty."[36] This affirmation of divine persistence completes the progressive, developmental, and eschatological orientation of Irenaean theodicy.

In the final analysis, then, Hick is not able to admit the existence of gratuitous evil. On this point, ironically, Irenaean theodicy falls back into agreement with Augustinian theodicy. Hick says that "the Kingdom of God will be an infinite, because eternal, good, outweighing all temporal and therefore finite evils."[37] Interestingly, whereas Augustinian theodicy argues for the possibility of evil in a theistic universe, Hick uses Irenaean theodicy to argue for its actuality being necessary to the kind of theistic universe he describes. So, Irenaean theodicy places the responsibility for evil on God in at least as strong a sense as Augustinian theodicy does. Yet in relation to the fulfillment of God's purpose, "nothing will finally have been sheerly and irredeemably evil. For everything will receive a new meaning in the light of the end to which it leads."[38]

Hick's contribution to the ongoing discussion of God and evil is an important one. He must be commended for not denying the reality of the evil in the world by saying that it only *seems* evil from our finite perspective. Although he tries to face even the most horrible and excessive evils, his theodicy cannot ultimately recognize really gratuitous evils. Even though, for Hick, it was within God's power to make a world significantly like this one but without dysteleological evils, such a world would not have been as conducive to soul-making as is this world. Thus, contrary to other remarks he makes along the way,[39] in the end Hick comes very close to arguing that our world, even with its most extreme evils, is the best possible one for achieving God's purpose of soul-making. For those whose intuitions run counter to this conclusion, perhaps we must say that it comes down to differing conceptions of goodness and what goodness would do regarding things that are within its power.

Whitehead's Process Theodicy

Each of the theodicies I have surveyed so far has ended up rejecting the factual premise of the argument from gratuitous evil. Yet some thinkers do not believe that denying gratuitous evil is a satisfactory response to the problem, although they see such a denial as a logical consequence of classical theistic commitments. They seek to develop a viable theodicy based on an alternative conception of deity. One important alternative to classical theism is found in the process philosophy of Alfred North Whitehead. Process philosophy assumes a different metaphysical picture of reality than does much traditional philosophical thought upon which classical theism rests. Process thinkers—such as Charles Hartshorne, John Cobb, and David Ray Griffin—have employed process concepts to articulate what is commonly known as *process theism* and its implications for theodicy. They claim that process theism retains the strengths of classical theism while avoiding its weaknesses and that there are clear benefits to theodicy.

Process thought is based on a view of reality as *becoming* rather than *being*, which is a direct reversal of the traditional approach. It is not surprising, then, that the central theme in process theodicy is the concept of change, development, evolution—both in the creaturely world and in God. Creatures are conscious, ever-changing centers of activity and experience rather than relatively enduring substances.[40] God, for process thought, has two natures: Primordial Nature and Consequent Nature. God's Primordial Nature contains all eternal possibilities for how the creaturely world can advance; God's Consequent Nature contains the experiences and responses of creatures as they choose to actualize some of these possibilities in their lives. As God's Consequent Nature changes in response to events in the creaturely world, God also may be said to change or to be in process—not something that classical theists would say of God. Although process thinkers deny that they hold a pantheistic worldview, the intimate and reciprocal ontological relationship between God and the world is obvious. Process thinkers have labeled their position "panentheism," which affirms that the experiences of the world are included in God.[41]

One key point in process theodicy is the rejection of the classical concept of divine omnipotence, which process thinkers find inadequate and laden with fallacies. Process theists deny that God has a monopoly on power or is "infinite in power," as traditional theology affirms. Since finite creatures are also centers of power (or "freedom" or "self-determination"), they can bring about new states of affairs that God cannot control. Although traditional theisms typically envision God choosing to bestow some degree of significant freedom on creatures, the process version of freedom is rooted in the very structure of reality, with each creature having the inherent power of self-determination. This power enables creatures to choose good or evil possibilities for their lives. God's power, then, can meet real resistance from creatures. Thus, we may say that God has all of the power that it is possible for a being to have but not all of the power that there is.

This marks a clear parting of the ways with the classical concept of omnipotence, which process theists criticize as monopolistic and totalitarian.[42]

According to process thinkers, God's chief goal for the universe is the realization and maximization of value in the experience of creaturely realities. Important values here include novelty, creativity, adventure, intensity, complexity, and so forth. But God's power must be viewed as *persuasive* rather than *coercive*. God tries to "persuade" or "lure" creatures toward the good and away from evil, but he cannot force them to choose the good. Process thinker David Ray Griffin states that God cannot eliminate evil because "God cannot unilaterally effect any state of affairs."[43] Instead, God offers persons possibilities for the realization of good in their experience. When negative ("evil") experiences occur, threatening to thwart the divine aim, God simply offers new ideal possibilities that are adjusted to what has already happened. Again, creatures freely respond, and again, God offers new possibilities. So goes the evolution of the world as God continually creates increased order and significance out of aboriginal chaos and triviality.

Since finite creatures are always perishing, process theodicy affirms that God is continually storing up their experiences in his Consequent Nature. All positive and negative experiences are ultimately conserved and harmonized in God's own conscious life. Thus, all things can be said to work out all right insofar as God "include[s] in himself a synthesis of the total universe."[44] In his function as "the Kingdom of Heaven," God brings about a kind of synthesis of all earthly experiences but does not unilaterally rectify all evils. Typically, process thinkers have not conceived of "personal immortality" or "life after death" as central to the defense of God's goodness against the problem of evil, as traditional Christian thinkers sometimes do.[45] There is also no final, definitive, eschatological culmination of all things. Thus, for process thinkers, the continual, ongoing synthesis of all experiences in God's own conscious life is the basic hope for the triumph of good and the redemption of the world.

Process theism has forced classical theists to rethink and refine their fundamental concepts.[46] But classical theists as well as some nontheists have also raised a number of serious objections to process thought. For example, the process attack on the classical concept of divine power has been said to rest on pure caricature that sets up an oversimplified "either/or" distinction between coercive and persuasive power. It is probably wiser to admit that there may be a range of modes of divine power, such as "productive power" or "sustaining power" or "enabling power," many of which are compatible with moral persuasion.[47] Another topic about which there is vigorous discussion is divine goodness. Some classical theistic thinkers declare that the process concept of God's goodness is fundamentally aesthetic rather than moral. If the aims of the process deity are to make creaturely experience richer and more complex, even at the cost of pain and discord, then there is the risk of violating many ordinary moral principles. Most classical theists understand that their own position denies that God could be morally perfect if he caused or allowed suffering in order to attain merely aesthetic aims. Process theists have replied that their conception of aesthetic value is a larger, more inclusive category than moral value. Hanging on the outcome of this dispute, of course, is the question of whether God is worthy of worship.

Putting these and other questions aside for the moment, let us focus on how process thought relates to the evidential argument from gratuitous evil. It would be difficult to think of another tradition in theodicy that tries to come to grips more squarely with what appear to be gratuitous evils in the world. In its analysis of the concept of power, process metaphysics makes room for really gratuitous evils. These are evils that God does not ordain, cannot control, and cannot necessarily make right. Now, in order to admit the existence of such evils, at the very least, process theists have radically overhauled the traditional theistic concept of divine power. They maintain that the classical concept of omnipotence leads logically to the denial of gratuitous evil and that their alternative concept of divine power allows us to acknowledge its existence.

In our brief survey of theodicies, it may seem that process thought has pushed us to a dilemma: *Either* we can retain classical categories and deny the existence of gratuitous evil *or* we can adopt process categories and accept gratuitous evil. In a sense, process theodicy defends theism against the argument from gratuitous evil by modifying theism—by opting for "quasi-theism," as it has been called. Thus, in terms of the historical discussion, the critic asks how classical theism deals with what appears to be gratuitous evil in the world. The process theist responds by conceding that classical theism cannot handle gratuitous evil and thus must be modified along process lines. Of course, for those theists who agree that there is something to the claim about gratuitous evil but who want to retain classical theistic commitments, the only visible option is to try to break the dilemma to which we have come. It may be that an interpretation of divine goodness and other divine attributes can be developed that allows for the possibility of genuinely gratuitous evil. But that is a project that lies beyond the scope of the present volume.[48]

Theodicy and the Assessment of Theism

The complete list of comprehensive theodicies as well as the various themes that they incorporate is too long to treat in this chapter. However, this sampling of approaches begins to acquaint us with the wide scope of moves available to theists and a number of counter-moves open to critics.

We can detect one common thread running through virtually all theistic solutions, whether global theodicies or more specific themes: *God (who is omnipotent, omniscient, and wholly good) would design the universe such that evil is necessary to a greater good.* Theists have typically taken a *greater-good approach* as integral to their search for a morally sufficient reason for why God allows evil. For many who think about the problem, it seems to be a deeply held intuition that for an evil to be justified—and for God to be justified in permitting it—the evil must be necessary to a greater good. If it were not strictly "necessary," then a God who is all-powerful, all-knowing, and all-good could achieve the specified good through other means. With this strategy in the background, theistic thinkers have proposed a variety of types of goods and a range of suggestions for how they are connected with evils. The various responses to evil in the immediately preceding pages only hint at the wide spectrum of possibilities.

Actually, the greater-good schema is also the common root of many defenses to the problem of evil. Using a greater-good approach defensively, many theists have long endorsed a greater-good strategy to undermine all versions of the logical problem of evil, for example. In constructing a defense around the theme of free will, theists have stated that the greater good of free will is a *possible* reason for why a deity who is supremely powerful and perfectly good allows evil. However, the greater-good strategy stands behind many attempts to develop a positive theodicy as well. The free will theme is one that theists have used in the context of theodicy, not as a merely *possible* reason for God's permission of evil but as a purportedly *true* and plausible reason. Whether it is free will or some other proposed greater good, let us focus here on the general strategy of specifying a greater good as the basis for theodicy.

Many theists and their critics believe that a morally sufficient reason for why God allows evil must relate evil to a good that outweighs it. These theists usually take for granted that no explanation of evil can be acceptable unless it credibly argues that the evil in question is necessarily connected to a greater good. A large number of theodicies, then, simply offer different ways of construing what that good is. In effect, they conclude that no existing evils are pointless or gratuitous and thus that they do not count as evidence against the existence of God. Here *gratuitous evil* is understood as an evil that is not necessary to the existence of a greater good. The most potent atheistic rebuttals to theistic specifications of greater goods revolve around the claim that at least some evils or some broad kinds of evil do not seem necessary to any greater good. It makes more sense to believe either that they serve no good purpose whatsoever or that the purpose they supposedly serve is not worth the price.

In the history of the debate over theodicy, several important points have been made by both sides. In future debates, perhaps critics could probe more deeply into the question of whether a greater-good justificatory scheme is viable. After all, attempting to justify evil by reference to some good essentially makes the moral weight of the evil depend on an extrinsic factor. It may well be, however, that a more promising line for the critic is to say that some actual evils are intrinsically so negative and destructive that no external good could outweigh them. This certainly is the tone of Ivan Karamazov's remarks to his brother Alyosha with which I opened this book. And the writings of Madden and Hare make a forceful case along these lines.

Theists, by contrast, could more fully explore a distinction between two sorts of greater-good theodicy: One type claims that the *actuality* of evil is necessary to a greater good, and another type claims that the *possibility* of evil is necessary to a greater good. Clearly, many of the unacceptable greater-good theodicies are of the first type. Following this first type of approach, theodicists embracing classical theism have to justify each actual evil or kind of evil by linking it to some actual good or class of goods—an effort that is extremely difficult and probably doomed. Some classical theists avoid many severe difficulties by denying that God is morally obligated to make each specific instance of evil turn out for the best, arguing instead that God is morally obligated to create or pursue a certain kind of world in which we have the potential for certain goods. A good kind of world would be structured according to certain overall policies. Such policies would include the granting of significant freedom to human beings, the establishment of a stable natural order, and so forth. These structural features of God's created order would then make many particular evils possible, evils that may or may not always be connected to particular goods within the world system, either now or in the future. According to this approach, the greater good would be the overall structure of the world order and the values that are generally able to emerge from it. Thus, as long as the theist describes a very valuable kind of world (structured so that free creatures can make significant choices, have the opportunity to develop moral character, and so on), the existence of such a world might well be seen as worth it.[49]

Ultimately, the dispute over evil is one of several considerations relevant to the rational acceptance or rejection of theistic belief. A reasoned judgment about the acceptability of theism, therefore, must be made in light of all of the relevant arguments for and against the existence of God. What is more, a final judgment would have to consider how well the overall theistic position fares in comparison to other worldviews, both religious and secular.

Notes

1. William Rowe, *Philosophy of Religion: An Introduction* (Encino and Belmont, Calif.: Dickenson, 1978), p. 88.

2. Edward Madden and Peter Hare, *Evil and the Concept of God* (Springfield, Ill.: Charles C. Thomas, 1968), p. 3.

3. Keith Yandell, *Basic Issues in the Philosophy of Religion* (Boston: Allyn and Bacon, 1971), pp. 62–63.

4. In the previous chapter, we considered Stephen Wykstra's defense, which turns on the cognitive limitations of human beings. Similar defenses are used by William Alston, "The Inductive Argument from Evil and the Human Cognitive Condition," in *The Evidential Argument from Evil*, ed. Daniel Howard-Snyder (Bloomington: Indiana University Press, 1996), pp. 97–125, and by Peter van Inwagen, "The Problem of Evil, the Problem of Air, and the Problem of Silence," in Howard-Snyder, pp. 151–174. Plantinga also alludes to the cognitive limitation theme: "Perhaps God has a good reason, but that reason is too complicated for us to understand"; see Alvin Plantinga, *God, Freedom, and Evil* (Grand Rapids, Mich.: Eerdmans, 1977), p. 10.

5. In other words, these theodicies offer a morally sufficient reason for God permitting evil.

6. This imagery is borrowed from Melville Stewart, *The Greater-Good Defense* (New York: St. Martin's, 1993), p. IX.

7. And whether for purposes of defense or theodicy, both agree that a Greater-Good Theme is needed. Since the theme is assumed to be necessary to theism, authors developing both defenses and theodicies employ it.

8. Augustine, *The Nature of the Good*, ed. and trans. J.H.S. Burleigh, in *Augustine: Earlier Writings* (London: S.C.M. Press, 1953), p. VI.

9. Interestingly, Neoplatonism heavily influenced Augustine's view of evil. For a discussion of Plotinian Neoplatonism, see W. R. Inge, *The Philosophy of Plotinus,* 3rd ed. (London: Longmans, Green, 1929). Plotinus's view of evil as lack occurs in Augustine, as explained in this chapter.

10. Friedrich Schleiermacher, *The Christian Faith* (Edinburgh: T. & T. Clark, 1928), p. 161.

11. Augustine, *City of God*, trans. Marcus Dods, George Wilson, and J. J. Smith (New York: Random House, 1950), pp. 13, 14.

12. Augustine, *Contra Julianum Pelagianum*, bk. 5, chap. 14.

13. To see how this principle is woven through much of Western intellectual history, see Arthur Lovejoy, *The Great Chain of Being* (Cambridge, Mass.: Harvard University Press, 1936).

14. John Hick, *Evil and the God of Love*, 2nd ed. (San Francisco: Harper & Row, 1978), pp. 82ff.

15. Augustine, *On Free Will*, trans. J.H.S. Burleigh, in *Augustine: Earlier Writings*, 3. 9. 26.

16. Augustine, *City of God*, 11. 23.

17. Augustine, *Enchiridion,* trans. J. F. Shaw, in *Basic Writings of St. Augustine* (2 vols.), ed., Whitney J. Oates (New York: Random House, 1948), .27

18. Ibid., 24. 96.

19. Ibid., 8. 27.

20. Gottfried Wilhelm von Leibniz, *Theodicy: Essays on the Goodness of God, the Freedom of Man, and the Origin of Evil*, trans. E. M. Huggard from C. J. Gerhardt's edition of the *Collected Philosophical Works* (1875–1890) (New Haven: Yale University Press, 1952).

21. Gottfried Wilhelm von Leibniz, *Theodicy*, trans. E. M. Huggard (London: Routledge & Kegan Paul, 1952), paras. 30–33.

22. Ibid., para. 201.

23. Ibid., para. 127.

24. Ibid., para. 9.

25. The reader will remember Plantinga's remarks on Leibniz's Lapse that was discussed in Chapter 3.

26. Hick, *Evil*, p. 255.

27. Ibid., p. 256.

28. Ibid., p. 281.

29. Ibid., p. 287.

30. Ibid., p. 272.

31. Ibid., pp. 329–330.

32. Hick speaks of "evil which is utterly gratuitous" (ibid., p. 324); of "evil in so far as it is purely and unambiguously evil" (ibid., p. 325); and "horrors which will disfigure the universe to the end of time" (ibid., p. 361).

33. Hick (ibid., p. 330) even quotes Shakespeare (*King Lear*): "As flies to wanton boys, are we to the gods, They kill us for their sport."

34. Ibid., p. 334.

35. Ibid., p. 176.

36. Ibid., p. 344.

37. Ibid., p. 350.

38. Ibid., p. 363.

39. Many of Hick's statements about the nature of evil indicate that sin and suffering are to be regarded as "genuinely *evil* and utterly inimical to God's will and purpose" (ibid., pp. 15–16); he also says: "For it is an inevitable deliverance of our moral consciousness, of which nothing must be allowed to rob us, that evil in all its forms is to be abhorred and resisted and feared" (ibid., p. 363).

40. Alfred North Whitehead, *Process and Reality* (New York: Macmillan, 1929), p. 343.

41. Michael Peterson, "God and Evil in Process Theodicy," in *Process Theology*, ed. Ronald Nash (Grand Rapids, Mich.: Baker Book House, 1987), p. 123.

42. See, for example, Charles Hartshorne, "Omnipotence," in *An Encyclopedia of Religion,* ed. V. Ferm (New York: Philosophical Library, 1945), pp. 545f. See also Charles Hartshorne, *Omnipotence and Other Theological Mistakes* (Albany: State University of New York Press, 1984), pp. 11f.

43. David Ray Griffin, *God, Power, and Evil* (Philadelphia: Westminster, 1976), p. 280.

44. Alfred North Whitehead, *Religion in the Making* (New York: Macmillan, 1926), p. 98; also see his *Process and Reality,* pp. 524–525.

45. Some process philosophers have attempted to provide a process account of personal immortality, that is, life after death. See the discussion of this in David Ray Griffin, *Evil Revisited: Responses and Reconsiderations* (Albany: State University of New York Press, 1991), pp. 34–40.

46. See the full-scale discussion of process theodicy in Peterson, "God and Evil in Process Theodicy," pp. 121–139.

47. Nancy Frankenberry, "Some Problems in Process Theodicy," *Religious Studies* 17 (1981): 181–184.

48. I suggested that Christian theists could take this kind of approach in my work *Evil and the Christian God* (Grand Rapids, Mich.: Baker Book House, 1982), particularly chap. 5, pp. 101–133. I also recommended it in the book I wrote with William Hasker, Bruce Reichenbach, and David Basinger, *Reason and Religious Belief: An Introduction to the Philosophy of*

Religion, 2nd ed. (New York: Oxford University Press, 1998), pp. 123–127. William Hasker makes a case for the possibility of gratuitous evil from the perspective of Christian theism in his "The Necessity of Gratuitous Evil," *Faith and Philosophy* 9 (1992): 23–44.

49. See Hasker, "Necessity"; Bruce Reichenbach, *Evil and a Good God* (New York: Fordham University Press, 1982); David Basinger, *The Case for Free Will Theism* (Downers Grove, Ill.: InterVarsity Press, 1996), chap. 4, pp. 83–104; and Peterson, *Evil and the Christian God.*

Suggested Readings

Adams, Marilyn M. "Theodicy Without Blame." *Philosophical Topics* 16 (Fall 1988): 215–245.

Adams, Marilyn M., advisory ed. Theological Contributions to Theodicy, special issue of *Faith and Philosophy* 13 (1996).

Basinger, David. "Divine Omnipotence: Plantinga vs. Griffin." *Process Studies* 11 (1981): 11–24.

Davis, Stephen T., ed. *Encountering Evil: Live Options in Theodicy.* Atlanta, Ga.: Knox Press, 1981.

Fales, Evan. "Antediluvian Theodicy: Stump on the Fall." *Faith and Philosophy* 6 (1989): 320–329.

———. "Should God Not Have Created Adam? *Faith and Philosophy* 6 (1992): 192–208.

Ferré, Nels. *Evil and the Christian Faith.* New York: Harper, 1947. Reprinted by Books for Libraries Press, New York, 1971.

Griffin, David Ray. *Evil Revisited: Responses and Reconsiderations.* Albany: State University of New York Press, 1991.

———. *God, Power, and Evil: A Process Theodicy.* Philadelphia: Westminster Press, 1976.

Hare, Peter. "Review of David Ray Griffin, *God, Power, and Evil.*" *Process Studies* 7 (1977): 44–51.

Hartshorne, Charles. "A New Look at the Problem of Evil." In *Current Philosophical Issues: Essays in Honor of Curt John Ducasse,* edited by F. C. Dommeyer. Springfield, Ill.: Charles C. Thomas, 1966, pp. 201–212.

Hasker, William. "Suffering, Soul-Making, and Salvation." *International Philosophical Quarterly* 28 (1988): 3–19.

Hick, John. *Evil and the God of Love.* 2nd ed. New York: Harper & Row, 1978.

———. "God, Evil and Mystery." *Religious Studies* 3 (1968): 539–546.

———. "The Problem of Evil in the First and Last Things." *Journal of Theological Studies* 19 (1968): 591–602.

Kane, G. Stanley. "The Concept of Divine Goodness and the Problem of Evil." *Religious Studies* 11 (1975): 49–71.

_____. "Evil and Privation." *International Journal for Philosophy of Religion* 11 (1980): 43–58.

_____. "The Failure of Soul-Making Theodicy." *International Journal for Philosophy of Religion* 6 (1975): 1–22.

_____. "Soul-Making Theodicy and Eschatology." *Sophia (Australia)* 14 (July 1975): 24–31.

Lewis, C. S. *The Problem of Pain*. New York: Macmillan, 1962.

Madden, Edward, and Peter Hare. *Evil and the Concept of God*. Springfield, Ill.: Charles C. Thomas, 1968.

Maritain, Jacques. *God and the Permission of Evil*. Milwaukee: Bruce Publishing, 1966.

Peterson, Michael. "God and Evil in Process Theology." In *Process Theology*, edited by Ronald Nash. Grand Rapids, Mich.: Baker Book House, 1987, pp. 117–139.

_____. "Recent Work on the Problem of Evil." *American Philosophical Quarterly* 20 (1983): 321–339.

Peterson, Michael, ed. *The Problem of Evil: Selected Readings*. Notre Dame, Ind.: University of Notre Dame Press, 1992.

Peterson, Michael, William Hasker, Bruce Reichenbach, and David Basinger. *Reason and Religious Belief: An Introduction to the Philosophy of Religion*. 2nd ed. New York: Oxford University Press, 1998, chap. 6, pp. 116–145.

Reichenbach, Bruce. *Evil and a Good God*. New York: Fordham University Press, 1982.

_____. "Natural Evils and Natural Law: A Theodicy for Natural Evils." *International Philosophical Quarterly* 16 (1976): 179–196.

Swinburne, Richard. "Does Theism Need a Theodicy?" *Canadian Journal of Philosophy* 18 (1988): 287–311.

_____. "Knowledge from Experience, and the Problem of Evil." In *The Rationality of Religious Belief: Essays in Honor of Basil Mitchell*, edited by William Abraham and Steven Holtzer. Oxford: Clarendon Press, 1987, pp. 141–167.

_____. "Natural Evil." *American Philosophical Quarterly* 15 (1978): 295–301.

_____. "The Problem of Evil." In *The Existence of God*. Oxford: Clarendon Press, 1979, pp. 200–224.

_____. "A Theodicy of Heaven and Hell." In *The Existence and Nature of God*, edited by Alfred Freddoso. Notre Dame, Ind.: Notre Dame University Press, 1983, pp. 37–54.

Whitney, Barry L. *Evil and the Process God*. New York: Mellen Press, 1985.

7

The Existential Problem of Evil

As noted earlier, the problem of evil may be divided into theoretical and existential dimensions. We are familiar with the various versions of the theoretical problem: the logical, probabilistic, and evidential formulations. Yet writers on the theoretical problem frequently allude to another kind of problem lying beyond the scope of the logical, probabilistic, and epistemic concerns that give shape to the various theoretical expressions. This other dimension of the problem of evil is more difficult to characterize. At the very least, it is rooted in the actual experience of evil and how that experience supports disbelief in God. It has been called a practical problem, a psychological problem, and a moral problem.[1] Alvin Plantinga has called it the "religious problem of evil,"[2] and Marilyn Adams has called it the "pastoral problem of evil."[3] What is clear is that, for some people, the existential feel for evil somehow leads to the rejection of religious belief.[4] Although there is no definitive study of the existential problem of evil, I shall explore major aspects of it here and tie together several important ideas about it from the current literature.

The Experience of Gratuitous Evil

What one might call the "phenomenology of evil"—that is, the study of the awareness of evil in human consciousness and how we assign meaning to it—is a rich field of investigation. Jeffrey Burton Russell insists that evil is "perceived immediately, directly and existentially."[5] Many other authors also believe that there is something forceful and primal about the way evil is experienced.[6] John Bowker writes that "the sheer bloody agonies of existence" are something of which "all men are aware and have direct experience."[7] Actually, it is not the experience of evil per se that has such intensity but the experience of evil *as* meaningless, pointless, gratuitous. It is this aspect of experience that is expressed in the bitter lament of the ordinary person as well as in the sophisticated reasoning of the antitheistic philosopher.[8] Great literature also provides extremely effective representations of this experience: Consider the writings of Dostoevsky,[9] Albert Camus,[10] and Miguel de Unamuno.[11]

There is something about the experience of evil as gratuitous that can and often does render faith in God untenable. Many persons say that they find themselves gripped at the core of their being by the horror of evil and that this awareness is profoundly transforming. Those who have this kind of perception of evil often report that they cannot experience the universe as theistic—that they could never manifest attitudes of praise, adoration, gratitude, and worship toward God. After reflecting on the horrible and absurd evils in the world that the divine being is supposed to allow, John Stuart Mill says, "When I am told that . . . I must . . . call this being by the names which express and affirm the highest human morality, I say in plain terms that I will not. Whatever power such a being may have over me, there is one thing which he shall not do: he shall not compel me to worship him."[12]

As long as theism is understood to entail that there are no gratuitous evils and as long as human beings experience much evil as gratuitous, then there will be a continuing tension between theistic belief and common experience. Some defensive maneuvers by theists such as Plantinga seek to show that the facts of evil do not render theism improbable. Other theists, such as Stephen Wykstra, argue defensively that we are in no position cognitively to affirm the existence (or likely existence) of gratuitous evil. In a sense, Plantinga sums up the net result of all such defensive strategies when he writes:

> The theist may find a *religious* problem in evil; in the presence of his own suffering or that of someone near to him he may find it difficult to maintain what he takes to be the proper attitude towards God. Faced with great personal suffering or misfortune, he may be tempted to rebel against God, to shake his fist in God's face, or even to give up belief in God altogether. But this is a problem of a different dimension. Such a problem calls not for philosophical enlightenment, but for pastoral care.[13]

So, presumably, at the strictly philosophical level—the level of logically reconciling various claims, confirming and disconfirming them—the critic's arguments can be staved off, and the intellectual doubts of believers can be assuaged. If there is any remaining objection to religious faith, then it must be emotional or attitudinal or practical in nature.

Plantinga correctly intimates that there is more to the problem of evil than abstract exercises in juggling propositions. But how we conceive of this other dimension in relation to the theoretical dimension is of major importance. To suggest that further philosophical enlightenment is not relevant to the attitudinal or experiential dimension bifurcates reason and experience. When defense against the problem of evil is coupled with Reformed epistemology, which affirms the theist's intellectual right to believe in God basically, many theists believe that virtually everything related to the issue of God and evil that is philosophically important has been addressed.

From another perspective, Marilyn Adams indicates that the pastoral or religious problem of evil "has a philosophical dimension in that it might be partially alleviated by some sort of explanations of how God is being good to created persons, even when he permits and/or causes evils such as these."[14] For Adams, to deny the bifurcation between theoretical considerations and the actual experience of evil is to move in a more appropriate direction. After all, there are many convincing philosophical and psychological studies, quite unrelated to the issue of God and evil, that argue for the intimate link between "logic and emotion" or "belief and experience." These studies show that what a person believes conditions the range and quality of his experience.[15]

It is not surprising that, in discussing the problem of evil, critic Sidney Hook observed that "no monotheistic religion which conceives of God as both omnipotent and benevolent, no metaphysic which asserts that the world is rational, necessary, and good has any room for genuine tragedy."[16] Here we may assume that Hook's term "genuine tragedy" refers to gratuitous evil. The point, then, is that what one believes about theism and its implications affects his experience of the world. We can see why theistic believers who understand the existence of God to exclude gratuitous evil would encounter significant dissonance in the face of intense experiences of evil as being gratuitous. John Hick captures something of this dissonance when he argues that a theology cannot be repugnant to the moral sense on which it is based.[17] In this same vein, we can comprehend why non-theists who ponder the credibility of theistic beliefs have great difficulty seeing how they fit with the experience of real life.

Adams is correct in suggesting that the religious problem can be somewhat alleviated by relevant explanations. In other words, a person's beliefs about God and their logical implications may need to be clarified, amplified, or modified. Or she may need to be encouraged, in an emotionally supportive context, to see that the beliefs she holds about God really call for attitudinal change or for a different personal response. Recognizing the seriousness of the religious problem, theologian Thomas Oden has articulated a "theodicy for pastoral practice." The pastoral approach Oden outlines clearly discounts false and harmful answers for evil, offers some general explanations for why evil exists, suggests how some good may still be brought out of unnecessary evil, and presents some general themes about God's love and care for persons in spite of the contingencies of human existence.[18]

One does not have to follow this sort of pastoral process very long to see that it cannot go far simply on the conceptual resources of restricted theism. Standard theistic beliefs about the divine attributes of omnipotence, omniscience, and perfect goodness imply only the broadest outlines of how to think about the relation of God and evil. Although sheer defense may be effectively based on restricted theism, any sufficient explanation of evil, which obviously takes us into the area of theodicy, requires additional resources, drawn from various doctrines and teachings of a faith tradition.

Evil and Personal Identity

We are now in a position to see how the experience of gratuitous evil supports the factual premise of the argument. For the person offering the argument from gratuitous evil, the factual claim—such as Rowe's (R1)—has strong experiential weight. Though the argument itself—its constituent propositions and their logical and epistemic relations—forms the theoretical dimension of the problem, it is intimately related to what we are calling the existential dimension. After all, the argument must be advanced by someone who thinks it is sound, that is, a person who believes the premises to be true and that they lead to the stated conclusion. We generally assume that the critic who believes there is gratuitous evil is expressing moral protest, indignation, and outrage. We typically see him as wishing violently that things were not the way they are and insisting that God, if he exists, is blameworthy for allowing them to be the way they are. That is a large part of the existential dimension of the problem.

But once a person experiences the world as containing gratuitous evils and is morally repulsed by their horrors, an interesting and subtle consideration arises. It is a deeply existential consideration pertaining to the person's value preferences toward himself and toward the world in general. According to a certain way of thinking about such things, a person can be *existentially authentic* or *existentially honest* in raising a theoretical statement of the problem of evil only if he genuinely regrets his own existence. This consideration provides the basis for an intriguing theistic response to the problem of gratuitous evil, a response that does not advance an explanatory theory of why God justifiably allows the evils of the world. Although it would be interesting to explore other nuances of the attitude of regret in relation to other statements of the problem of evil, I will focus here on the most formidable of all statements: the argument from gratuitous evil.

The particular theistic strategy here rests on certain value preferences or attitudes. The first step in developing this response is to call upon each individual who thinks about it—in this case, the atheist advancing the problem of gratuitous evil—to declare his attitude toward his own existence. William Hasker straightforwardly poses a question to each person who might advance the problem of evil as a reason for rejecting theism: *Am I glad that I exist?* He explains the exact meaning of the question as follows:

> The question is not whether my life is all that it ought to be or all that it conceivably could be. It is not whether the pleasure-pain balance in my life to date has been, on the whole, favorable or unfavorable. It is not whether my life is, in general, a benefit to those who are affected by it. It is not even the question whether my life, all things considered, contains more good than evil. All of these questions are deeply interesting, and the answers to them, if known, might affect my answer to the question which I am asking. But the question is simply, am I glad that I am alive? Or is my existence, on the whole, something which I regret? Is my life something which I *affirm*, or do I wish, like Job, that I had never been?[19]

Obviously, this casts the matter in a person-relative way. Each person must answer for himself whether he is glad for his own existence or would rather it be replaced by nonexistence. And the question can obviously be extended to ask whether one is glad for the existence of loved ones: *Am I glad of their existence?*

The second step in laying out the theistic existential response is to clarify what is necessary for human beings to exist as the unique individuals that they are. Hasker proposes a thesis that is not uncontroversial but is widely accepted by thinkers who hold a variety of philosophical perspectives. The thesis is

> (50) A necessary condition of my coming-into-existence is the coming-into-existence of my body.[20]

In one way or another, then, my unique personal identity depends somehow on having this particular body. Materialists, identity theorist, epiphenomenalists, behaviorists, and even Thomists accept this thesis. Cartesian dualists and the like, who do not hold that the body is a necessary condition of personal existence, will not feel the force of the following reasoning.

The third step in progressively unfolding this existential response is to show that, logically, whatever is necessary for *my body's* existence is necessary for *my* existence. That is, if my body is necessary for me to have individual personal existence, then whatever is necessary for my body's existence is also necessary for my personal existence. This principle, of course, holds for any person. When one honestly and thoroughly examines all of the necessary conditions for one's bodily existence, the results are impressive. In order for my body to come into existence, my parents would have had to have had a child. Had my mother married someone else, none of their children could have been *me*, since none of their bodies could have been *this* body. Moreover, not just any child of my parents would have been me, with my identical genetic heritage donated by a specific pair of male and female reproductive cells at a specific time.

All of this means that the coming into existence of any particular individual is, antecedently, an extremely improbable event. In fact, antecedently, it is quite improbable that any given individual would come into existence in view of his or her dependence on a multitude of other highly improbable events, such as the fortuitous circumstances surrounding how one's parents met and got married, which could include events as routine as a school prom or as dramatic as a world war. And behind one's parents stand a whole series of their progenitors, persons whose coming-into-being must have depended on yet other contingent events. All of this leads Hasker to conclude that

(51) Had major or significant events in the world's past history been different than they were, then in all probability neither I nor the persons whom I love would even have existed.

This secures the connection between one's attitude toward one's existence and the world's total history.

The meeting and mating of our ancestors was influenced by the events of their times—many of which were undoubtedly calamitous, such as wars, epidemics, crimes, accidents, and so forth. And we already know that no person has any reason whatever to suppose that he would have existed had the course of the world's history been substantially different. We are now in a position to grasp the link between one's individual existence and the existence of all the evils of the world leading up to his coming-into-being. As Robert Adams observes, "The farther back we go into history, the larger the proportion of evils to which we owe our being; for the causal nexus relevant to our individual genesis widens as we go back in time. We almost certainly would never have existed had there not been just about the same evils as actually occurred in a large part of human history."[21] Let us now explore the bearing of this link on the original question, *Am I glad that I exist?*

The Logic of Regret

At this point, we need to specify some principles governing the logical relationships between certain attitudes. The relevant attitudes are expressed by the phrases "being glad that" and "being sorry that." Such attitudes cannot be true or false, as beliefs are. Hasker contends that they share with beliefs, moral judgment, and imperatives the property of being *rationally consistent or inconsistent*. The sense of "glad" and "sorry" with which we are concerned is not essentially a matter of *feeling* gladness or sorrow, although it might involve these feelings. These attitudes are largely defined by *preference*. Thus, my being glad that P entails my *preferring* that P be the case rather than not-P. Conversely if I am *sorry* or *regret* that P, this means that I *would prefer* that not-P be the case rather than P. (Here P stands for the sentence that expresses the proposition that P, and P is the name of the state of affairs such that *P*.) By virtue of these preferences, the attitudes in question are rationally consistent or inconsistent.

At this point, we can begin to discern important logical principles that apply to the attitudes in question. Surely, we can say that

(52) If I am glad that P, I rationally cannot be sorry that P.

Of course, a person may *feel* both gladness and sorrow about something. This is what we mean when we say that an event in life is "bittersweet" (e.g., a parent whose child is getting married may be described as "being sad" that a family member is leaving home but "being glad" that she is finding committed companionship). But "being glad" in the relevant sense here involves an attitude of preference to which principle (52) applies.

Let us now specify some key definitions that will enable us to see the significance of some other important principles. Hasker first suggests this:

> 'A is *circumstantially glad* that P' = df 'A is glad that P, and there is some state-of-affairs *Q* such that A knows that if *Q* did not obtain neither would *P*, and A regrets that Q.'

One may, for example, be circumstantially glad that the University of Kentucky defeated the University of Utah to win the 1998 NCAA basketball championship but not prefer Kentucky's victory *under all possible circumstances* (i.e., on the whole). For example, one may have placed a large bet on Utah or believe that the NCAA's existence is a bad thing because its championships, television contracts, and the like foster corruption and an undue emphasis on athletics in our society. So, *given the circumstances*, one may be glad for Kentucky's victory. But this does not mean that one is glad on the whole. We are now ready for the second definition we need:

> 'A is *glad on the whole* that P' = df 'A is glad that P, and for any state-of-affairs *Q* such that A knows that if *Q* did not obtain neither would *P*, A is glad that Q.'

Modifying our example, we may say that one may be glad on the whole when, recognizing that the NCAA involves some undesirable consequences, he still definitely prefers Kentucky's championship victory. Finally, we may say that a person *regrets on the whole* that P whenever he is clearly *not* glad on the whole that P or is only circumstantially glad that P.

In light of these definitions, we can now see the significance of the following principle:

(53) If I am glad on the whole that P, and I know that *P* entails *Q*, then I rationally must be glad on the whole that Q.

And

(54) If I am glad on the whole that P, and I know that if *Q* did not obtain neither would *P*, then I rationally must be glad that Q.

These principles seem quite clearly correct. But when principle (54) is combined with (51) from the previous section regarding self-identity, we get an astounding conclusion:

(55) If I am glad on the whole about my own existence and that of those whom I love, then I must be glad that the history of the world, in its major aspects, has been as it has.

Of course, this conclusion does not follow deductively from (54) and (51) as they have been stated. Principle (54) speaks of my *knowing* that if *Q* did not obtain neither would *P*, whereas (51) says only that *in all probability* there is such a connection. This should make little difference in our attitude toward (55).[22] Perhaps, then, the reason why (55) has been largely ignored is the fact that (50) and (51) are not obvious. The ideas expressed in (54) and (55) have been discussed in philosophical literature. Benedict de Spinoza, for example, says that our ordinary judgments of good and evil are irrational precisely because in making them, we overlook the necessary connections between events.[23]

Existential Authenticity and Evil

If what we have said so far is sound and if the truth of (55) has been established, what bearing does all this have for the problem of evil? Put more precisely, what effect can it have on one who advances or considers advancing the argument from gratuitous evil? For a person who is glad on the whole that he exists or even that someone he loves exists, then it follows—due to (55) above—that he must be glad also about the world's existence and about the general course its history has taken. But then it is very difficult for him to be *existentially authentic* or *existentially honest* in advancing the argument from gratuitous evil. Let us see why this is so.

The argument from gratuitous evil involves affirming a factual premise about there being evil in the world that serves no good purpose. To have the experiential grounds for affirming this crucial premise is to have certain moral convictions, to consult one's experience of the goods and evils of life, and to be morally repulsed by what one finds. To assert the factual premise is, in effect, to issue a complaint that there is something drastically wrong with the world as a whole. And we now are keenly aware of the intricate causal interconnections between all the events in the world (including evil events) and our own existence. Thus, the critic who is glad on the whole for his own existence or that of those whom he loves cannot be existentially authentic in advancing the factual premise. Robert Adams writes: "The fact that we owe our existence to evils gives rise to a problem of evil, not only for theists but for anyone who loves an actual human individual—himself or anyone else. How is our love for actual human selves to be reconciled with moral repudiation of the evils that crowd the pages of history? Are we to wish that neither we nor the evils had existed?"[24]

Based on this line of reasoning, the following existential stance simply becomes ludicrous:

(56) The world as we know it is morally so objectionable that a God who tolerated it could in no meaningful sense be called good—nevertheless, *I am glad for my own existence and therefore I am also glad that the world exists and that the main events and features of its history have been as they have.*

We may say that such a posture is *existentially self-stultifying* or *existentially self-defeating*.

It should now be intuitively evident that

(57) If I am glad on the whole about my own existence and that of persons close to me, then I cannot reproach God for the general character or the major events of the world's past history.

Since reproach is attitudinal, preferential, and existential in nature, the critic is hereby blocked from reproaching God by citing the general character and major events of the past, many of which were tragic for the persons involved. It will also not do for the critic to base his argument from gratuitous evil just on events in his own lifetime, events, therefore, on which his own existence does not depend in the way in which it depends on those tragic events of the past. After all, the tragedies of our lifetime are simply the same *kinds* of events as those that have occurred countless times in the past. For a critic to mount his moral complaint solely on the basis of evil events that occur only in his lifetime is for him to express a position too egocentric to deserve serious attention.

Thus, the critic who is positively glad about (i.e., does not positively regret) his own existence cannot advance the general problem of gratuitous evil in an existentially authentic way. One interesting aspect of this approach to the existential problem is that, without trying to sketch an overall view of why God allows evil, it strikes on a very deep level at one's sense of existence. Furthermore, it logically connects one's existence with the overall state of the world. This response capitalizes on an often neglected fact: that we do not come to our judgments about the goodness or badness of existence from the standpoint of "a cosmic ideal observer." This is a standpoint we can never attain. Instead, each of us comes to these judgments from a personal standpoint as an existing human being—one who prospers and struggles, rejoices and sorrows, laughs and weeps, and is glad for the opportunity to live out his life upon the earth. It is the critic who adopts *this* standpoint who cannot raise the problem of gratuitous evil in an existentially authentic way.

There are, of course, other types of critics who are glad that they exist and yet are not deterred by the preceding line of reasoning. One type would be the antitheistic critic who is indeed glad on the whole that she exists or that her loved ones exist and who conceives and presents the problem of evil merely as a matter of internal inconsistency for theistic belief (as explored in Chapter 2). Another type of critic may take the problem of evil to be a probabilistic difficulty for theistic belief in light of evil in the world (as explored in Chapter 4). In either case, the critics in question need not support any substantive premises, commit to any moral principles, or form any value judgments about the actual state of the world. So, the theistic response here does not directly address them. Of course, we have already seen that the logical and probabilistic arguments from evil are vulnerable to rebuttal in other ways. As shown in Chapter 5, the argument from gratuitous evil is the most difficult for the theist to rebut anyway. Chapter 6 reviewed several theodicies that could be interpreted as attempts to answer the argument from gratuity by offering theoretical explanations. But now we see a different way for the theist to respond to the antitheistic critic who advances the argument.

This still leaves us with the one very formidable type of critic—the person who is willing to say that he positively *regrets* his own existence on the whole. This is the person—presumably a very rare individual indeed—who is able honestly to say that he would truly wish and would prefer that some other world, in which no one now living has a share, or perhaps no world at all should exist in place of this present evil world of which he is unhappily a part. Out of the depths of his own pointless suffering, the ancient patriarch Job cursed the day of his birth:

"Let the day perish in which I was born, and the night that said, 'A man-child is conceived.'

"Let that day be darkness! May God above not seek it, or light shine on it.

"Let gloom and deep darkness claim it. Let clouds settle upon it; let the blackness of the day terrify it.

"That night—let thick darkness seize it! let it not rejoice among the days of the year; let it not come into the number of the months.

"Yes, let that night be barren; let no joyful cry be heard in it.

"Let those curse it who curse the Sea, those who are skilled to rouse up Leviathan.

"Let the stars of its dawn be dark; let it hope for light, but have none; may it not see the eyelids of the morning—

"because it did not shut the doors of my mother's womb, and hide trouble from my eyes.

"Why did I not die at birth, come forth from the womb and expire?

"Why were there knees to receive me, or breasts for me to suck?

"Now I would be lying down and quiet; I would be asleep; then I would be at rest

"with kings and counselors of the earth who rebuild ruins for themselves,

"or with princes who have gold, who fill their houses with silver.

"Or why was I not buried like a stillborn child, like an infant that never sees the light?"[25]

This is the deep existential regret that is required for one meaningfully to raise the argument from gratuitous evil. To be able to assert the factual premise that there is gratuitous evil, the critic must positively *regret* on the whole that he, his family, his friends, all his loved ones, and all the rest of us have ever lived.

Perhaps Ivan Karamazov is the paradigmatic figure here. Ivan resists his brother's declaration that all events in the world contribute to a divinely designed "higher harmony" that will be revealed at the end of time:

> You see, Alyosha, perhaps it really may happen that if I live to that moment, or rise again to see it, I, too, perhaps may cry aloud with the rest, looking at the mother embracing the child's torturer, "Thou art just, O Lord!" but I don't want to cry aloud then. While there is still time, I hasten to protect myself and so I renounce the higher harmony altogether. It's not worth the tears of that one tortured child who beat itself on the breast with its little fist and prayed in its stinking outhouse, with its unexpiated tears to "dear, kind God"! It's not worth it, because those tears are unatoned for.[26]

Summarizing his existential posture, Ivan declares, "In the final result, I don't accept this world of God's, and, although I know it exists, I don't accept it at all."[27]

Here we have a person who is willing to say that the existence and history of the world has not been worth it. For Ivan, many of the world's evils are gratuitous because whatever purpose they serve is not worth the price. A rebellious existential hero, Ivan clearly seems ready to embrace the implication that he must be willing for his own existence to be replaced by nonexistence. What Ivan does, then, is to answer the penetrating question with which we have been working— *Am I glad that I exist?*—and to answer it negatively. This answer allows him to be existentially honest or authentic in rejecting the evils of the world.[28] It is these kinds of persons—the Ivan Karamazovs of this world—who are unaffected by the theistic response to the problem of evil that has been sketched here. Ivan is the person who can honestly say that he regrets his own existence and the existence of all whom he loves, since too great a price in terms of misery and suffering has been paid for their existence.[29]

In fact, for such a person, framing his objection in terms of the general problem of gratuitous evil is somewhat unnecessary because he can consider the evils occurring in his own life as the only factual instance of gratuity he needs to cite. On that basis alone, he might object that the God of theism does not exist. Or he might cite as a case in point any single life that does not seem to be good on the whole, not a great good to the person living it. An implicit assumption here would be that a morally good deity would not allow even one individual to have a life that is not a great good to him on the whole, regardless of what broad reasons there are for thinking that our world is good on balance. This line of thought, of course, pursues the attack in an Ivan-like direction. And it certainly makes the attempt to apply general explanations for evils to individual cases impertinent, at least, and damaging, at most.[30]

The Defeat of Horrendous Evil

It is not clear whether restricted theism offers enough rich ideas to fashion an effective response to the person who says that he regrets his own existence or that of the whole world. The critic's charge here is essentially that it would have been better if God—if he exists at all—had not created this world. For one thing, the theist might query, "Better *for whom*?" since if God had not created this world and the critic had not come into existence, it could hardly be better for the critic. For another thing, the theist who accepts the fact of gratuitous evil in a theistic universe may stress the overall value of the moral enterprise—even if there are no guarantees that all evils will always be compensated with greater goods. But all such tactics may still be met with the Ivan-like response, "Ah, but what about all the horrendous suffering? It is just not worth it. Nothing can make it worth it." Ivan even admits that all people may indeed be resurrected at the end of time and that victims may forgive their torturers. But that will all be too unjust, he insists, since some of the sufferings are too awful to be compensated.[31] For Ivan, there are too many people whose lives are not a great good to them and may, on balance, not have positive value. Thus, no just and loving deity could have created a world that contains them. Put another way, the magnitude of the horrific evils that some tragic human lives include cannot be even approximately estimated without recognizing that they are incommensurate with any collection of goods.

Although we are entering a territory of fundamental disagreement between the theist and critic, a territory that is largely uncharted, Marilyn Adams has offered a response that is distinctively Christian as well as theistic. She observes that most responses to the problem of evil are generic (specifying a general reason for evil) and global (focusing on some feature of the world that makes evil possible). Yet she points out the insufficiency of generic and global solutions for the problem raised by horrendous evils. "Horrendous evils" are evils the doing or suffering of which gives one prima facie reason to doubt whether one's life could (given the inclusion of such evils in it) be a great good to one on the whole. Adams argues that the attribute of divine goodness must be analyzed to show not only that God would create a world that is good on the whole but also that he would not allow any individual lives to be lived that are engulfed and overcome by evil. The difficulty that the Christian theist faces here is not only that do we not know God's *actual* reason for permitting horrendous evils but also that we cannot even *conceive* of any plausible reasons.[32]

Employing what she calls the "resources of religious value theory," Adams develops an argument that horrendous evils can be defeated in the context of the lives of individuals who experience them. Let us simply say that evil is "defeated" when it is part of a life that is good on the whole, when it is related appropriately to relevant and great goods. Adams agrees with rebels like Ivan Karamazov and John Stuart Mill in insisting that there is no set of temporal and finite goods that can guarantee that a person whose life includes horrendous evils will be a great good to him or her on the whole.

According to Adams, it is the intimate relationship with God that has value incommensurable with anything else:

> From a Christian point of view, God is a being a greater than which cannot be conceived, a good incommensurate with both created goods and temporal evils. Likewise, the good of beatific, face-to-face intimacy with God is simply incommensurate with any merely non-transcendent goods or ills a person might experience. Thus, the good of beatific face-to-face intimacy with God would *engulf* . . . even the horrendous evils humans experience in this present life here below, and overcome any prima-facie reasons the individual had to doubt whether his/her life would or could be worth living.[33]

The central logic at work here is that the worst evils demand to be defeated by the best goods.[34] Christian theists such as Marilyn Adams argue, then, that horrendous evils can be overcome only by the infinite goodness of God.

Adams claims that it is not necessary to find reasons (even merely logically possible reasons) *why* God might permit horrendous evils. Thus, theoretical theodicy is not essential. It is enough for the Christian theist to show *how* God can be good enough to created persons despite their participation in such horrors. For Christian theists to show this, according to Adams, they must work out the implications of divine goodness conceived not just as aiming at the excellent production of global goods but also as not allowing any individual life to sustain evils that would ultimately engulf it. Her conclusion, then, is that, for a person who experiences horrendous evil, God can ensure that his life is a great good to him only by integrating participation in those evils into a personal relationship with God himself. This is, in effect, to offer a practical or existential theodicy.

How shall we think about what it means for God to integrate horrendous evil into a relationship with himself? Adams argues that God's loving identification with the sufferer, vividly displayed in his own self-sacrifice in the person of Jesus of Nazareth, is a helpful Christian model in this context.[35] She asserts that Christian theism teaches that God through Christ participated in horrendous evil, experiencing human horrors. Thus, the sufferer can identify (either sympathetically or mystically) with Christ and thereby have access to the inner life of God. According to Adams, this experience of God preempts the need to know why horrendous evils exist.[36] At the end of his long ordeal with anguish and loss, the biblical character Job was not privileged to know the reasons why he suffered so terribly. But he was given an intimate vision of God that seemed to satisfy him and let him see that his life was indeed a great good. Job answered the Lord: "I know that you can do all things, and that no purpose of yours can be thwarted. I have uttered what I did not understand, things too wonderful for me, which I did not know. I had heard of you by the hearing of the ear, but now my eye sees you."[37]

In the final analysis, the issue comes down to whether Adams's case is acceptable to the one to whom it is addressed. Adams can maintain that her own distinctively Christian approach is internally consistent, although the Christian theist and the critic will predictably differ on the truth and plausibility of its claims. The antitheistic critic, by contrast, could agree that God, if he exists, is a good incommensurable with all other goods. But he might object that some means by which people can be connected to God (e.g., horrendous suffering) are so intrinsically awful that they still violate other moral principles we hold. The critic might also complain that Adams has shifted ground in answering the theoretical problem by giving a practical solution. The critic might even press the point that it is extremely difficult to understand what it is for one person to experience another's pain or for suffering to be an avenue of interpersonal identification and thus that the acceptability of Adams's answer hangs, in part, on fuller analysis of such concepts. Adams and other Christian theists may eventually offer complete accounts of these concepts so that this strand of existential theodicy may advance. It is hard to say exactly where the future discussion of the existential problem of evil will lead, but it is sure to be both fascinating and important.

Notes

1. Kenneth Surin distinguishes theoretical from practical problems of evil in his *Theology and the Problem of Evil* (Oxford: Blackwell, 1986), p. 112. Robert Adams calls it a psychological problem in his *The Virtue of Faith and Other Essays in Philosophical Theology* (New York: Oxford University Press, 1987), p. 75. William Hasker alludes to the problem being a form of moral protest in "On Regretting the Evils of this World," *Southern Journal of Philosophy* 19 (1981): 425.

2. Alvin Plantinga, *God, Freedom, and Evil* (Grand Rapids, Mich.: Eerdmans, 1977), p. 63.

3. Marilyn Adams, "Redemptive Suffering: A Christian Solution to the Problem of Evil," in *The Problem of Evil: Selected Readings,* ed. Michael L. Peterson (Notre Dame, Ind.: University of Notre Dame Press, 1992), p. 171.

4. Edward Madden and Peter Hare, *Evil and the Concept of God* (Springfield, Ill.: Charles C. Thomas, 1968), p. 25.

5. Jeffrey Burton Russell, "The Experience of Evil," *Listening* 9 (1974): 72.

6. Paul Ricouer, *The Symbolism of Evil,* trans. Emerson Buchanan (Boston: Beacon Press, 1967); see, for instance, pp. 3–5.

7. John Bowker, *Problems of Suffering in Religions of the World* (London: Cambridge University Press, 1970), p. 2.

8. A contemporary classic, written for the layperson, that expresses grief and bitterness in a struggle to maintain religious faith is C. S. Lewis's, *A Grief Observed* (New York: Macmillan, 1961). Another book in the same spirit is Nicholas Wolterstorff, *Lament for a Son* (Grand Rapids, Mich.: Eerdmans, 1987).

9. Fyodor Dostoevsky, *The Brothers Karamazov,* trans. Constance Garnett (New York: Norton, 1976), particularly pp. 217–227.

10. Almost all of Albert Camus's writings can be seen as dealing with the problem of gratuitous evil and the senseless destruction of things of value. But see particularly his "The Myth of Sisyphus," in *The Myth of Sisyphus and Other Essays,* trans. Justin O'Brien (New York: Alfred A. Knopf, 1955), pp.

1–138. Also see Camus, *The Plague,* trans. Stuart Gilbert (New York: Alfred A. Knopf, 1948).

11. Miguel de Unamuno, *The Tragic Sense of Life,* trans. J. Crawford Flitch (New York: Dover, 1954).

12. From John Stuart Mill, "The Philosophy of the Conditioned as Applied by Mr. Mansel to the Limits of Religious Thought," in *An Examination of Sir William Hamilton's Philosophy,* reprinted in Nelson Pike, ed., *God and Evil: Readings on the Theological Problem of Evil* (Englewood Cliffs, N.J.: Prentice-Hall, 1964), p. 43.

13. Plantinga, *God, Freedom, and Evil,* pp. 63–64.

14. M. Adams, "Redemptive Suffering," p. 171.

15. Edward Walter, "The Logic of Emotions," *Southern Journal of Philosophy* 10 (1972): 71–78.

16. Sidney Hook, "Pragmatism and the Tragic Sense of Life," *Proceedings and Addresses of the American Philosophical Association* (October 1960), reprinted in Robert Corrigan, ed., *Tragedy: Vision and Form* (San Francisco: Chandler, 1965), p. 68.

17. John Hick, *Evil and the God of Love,* 2nd ed. (San Francisco: Harper & Row, 1978), p. 92.

18. Thomas Oden, "A Theodicy for Pastoral Practice," in his *Pastoral Theology* (San Francisco: Harper & Row, 1983), pp. 223–248.

19. Hasker, "Regretting," pp. 425–426.

20. Ibid., p. 427. Here I have renumbered Hasker's principles for the sake of continuity in the context of this book. All remaining principles cited here may be found in the context of Hasker's articles and will not carry further references.

21. Robert M. Adams, "Existence, Self-Interest, and the Problem of Evil," in his *Virtue of Faith,* p. 66.

22. Hasker, "Regretting," p. 431. Hasker writes: "Note first of all that, given the truth of (A), it is *certain,* and not just probable, that subsequent to any major calamity, such as a war, many of the persons who come into existence are different individuals from those who would have existed had the calamity not occurred. Many persons who would otherwise have become parents die without having children. Those who would have been their mates have children with other partners, and so on. Within a few generations, it is likely that hardly anyone living in the affected area is identical with any individual who would have existed, had the calamity not occurred. What is more difficult is to show that this is true in the case of a given individual. But even in the individual case, the probabilities mount up very rapidly. Suppose, for example, that had the First World War not occurred there is one chance in ten that my parents would have met each other. (I am sure that this is too high. But at this point I can afford to be conservative.) Suppose, furthermore, that on just two previous occasions the meeting and mating of

some of my earlier ancestors has been influenced in similar ways by calamitous events of their own times. Then neglecting all other factors (all of which, if considered, would further strengthen my argument), the likelihood of my existing, if just these three major calamities had not occurred, is no better than one in a thousand! The truth is, that I have no reason whatever to suppose that I would have existed, had the course of the world's history been substantially different. But what I have no reason to suppose true must for practical purposes be disregarded. So (55) must be accepted."

23. Benedict de Spinoza, *Ethics,* ed. Henry Frowde, trans. W. Hale White. Revised by Amelia Hutchinson Stirling (London: Oxford University Press, 1910), pp. 80–81.

24. R. Adams, "Existence," p. 75.

25. Job 3:3–7 New Revised Standard Version.

26. Ivan Karamazov in Dostoevsky, *The Brothers Karamazov*, p. 225.

27. Ibid., p. 216.

28. We note here but cannot pursue the well-known case of Leo Tolstoy who came to the conclusion that life had no meaning and was not worth living and thus came to the brink of suicide. If the critic raising the problem of gratuitous evil is willing to say that he regrets his own existence, that his own existence is not a positive good to him on the whole, then the theist might ask why he does not commit suicide. What we might call the suicide argument seems especially strong for the one who is willing to say he regrets his existence. See Leo Tolstoy, *My Confessions,* trans. Leo Wiener (London: J. M. Dent, 1905).

29. Although we cannot explore the matter here, the reality of suffering and the search for the proper response to the awareness of suffering lies at the heart of Buddhism. Nirvana (nonexistence) is recommended. See John Bowker, *Problems of Suffering in Religions of the World* (Cambridge: Cambridge University Press, 1970), pp. 237–258.

30. The tendency of certain theodical answers to do damage to persons is discussed in Terrence W. Tilley, *The Evils of Theodicy* (Washington, D.C.: Georgetown University Press, 1991).

31. Ivan Karamazov in Dostoevsky, *The Brothers Karamazov*, pp. 224–226.

32. M. Adams, "Horrendous Evils and the Goodness of God," *Proceedings of the Aristotelian Society*, supplementary vol. 63 (1989): 297–310. The present quote is from the reprinted piece in Robert Merrihew Adams and Marilyn McCord Adams, eds., *The Problem of Evil* (New York: Oxford University Press, 1990), p. 215.

33. M. Adams, "Horrendous Evils," p. 218. The reader should consult the complete article for technical distinctions between *balancing off, defeating,* and *engulfing* evil.

34. Tolstoy (mentioned in Note 28) came to accept this kind of logic: that only the infinite can give meaning to the finite. Thus, he averted suicide and claimed to find meaning in his life.

35. M. Adams, "Redemptive Suffering," pp. 169–187.
36. M. Adams, "Horrendous Evils," p. 220.
37. Job 42:2, 3b, 5 New Revised Standard Version.

Suggested Readings

Adams, Marilyn M. "Horrendous Evils and the Goodness of God." *The Aristotelian Society: Supplementary Volume* 63 (1989): 297–310.

_____. "Problems of Evil: More Advice to Christian Philosophers." *Faith and Philosophy* 5 (1988): 121–143.

_____. "Redemptive Suffering: A Christian Solution to the Problem of Evil." In *Rationality, Religious Belief, and Moral Commitment,* edited by Robert Audi and William J. Wainwright. Ithaca: Cornell University Press, 1986, pp. 248–267.

Adams, Robert M. "Existence, Self-Interest, and the Problem of Evil." *Nous* 13 (1979): 53–65.

Dupré, Louis. "Evil—A Religious Mystery." *Faith and Philosophy* 7 (1990): 261–280.

Hasker, William. "On Regretting the Evils of This World." *Southern Journal of Philosophy* 19 (1981): 425–437.

Hauerwas, Stanley. *Naming the Silences: God, Medicine, and the Problem of Suffering.* Grand Rapids, Mich.: Eerdmans, 1990.

_____. *Suffering Presence: Theological Reflections on Medicine, the Mentally Handicapped, and the Church.* Notre Dame, Ind.: University of Notre Dame Press, 1985.

Kohák, Erazim. "The Person in a Personal World: An Inquiry into the Metaphysical Significance of the Tragic Sense of Life." *Independent Journal of Philosophy* 1 (1977): 51–64.

Lewis, C. S. *The Problem of Pain.* New York: Macmillan, 1962.

Peterson, Michael. "Recent Work on the Problem of Evil." *American Philosophical Quarterly* 20 (1983): 321–339.

Peterson, Michael, ed. *The Problem of Evil: Selected Readings.* Notre Dame, Ind.: University of Notre Dame Press, 1992.

Index

Printed in the United States
40342LVS00006B/145